IF GOD CARES SO MUCH WHY DO I STILL HURT?

If God Cares So Much

WHY DO I STILL HURT?

A PRACTICAL SPIRITUAL GUIDE TO HAPPINESS

Kerie Boshka

IF GOD CARES SO MUCH, WHY DO I STILL HURT?
A PRACTICAL SPIRITUAL GUIDE TO HAPPINESS

Published by   AARK House Publishing, LLC.
                  1127 High Ridge Road #295
                  Stamford, CT 06905

AARK House Publishing titles may be purchased for business or promotional use or for special sales. For information, please write to: Special Markets Department, AARK House Publishing, 1127 High Ridge Road #295, Stamford, CT 06905.

Printed in the United States of America

Cover design by Christine Grace
Interior book design by HRoberts Design, Inc.
Cover photography by Jamie Collins Photography

First Printing: January 2011
ISBN- 978-0-615-43186-4
Library of Congress Control Number: 2010919153

For Tommy and Rick,
who changed my life forever.

Acknowledgments

My sincerest thanks to:

Gay Walley, my amazing writing coach and true partner on this book. Without you, I never would have found the courage, or the skill, to complete this project. You brought the writer in me to life. I can never thank you enough. [www.nycwritingcoach.com]

My editors, Joanne Zazzaro and Rachel Craig. Your incredible insight and skill shaped this book into a presentable manuscript.

My cover design team—my go-to photographer Jamie Collins, whose creativity and energy is unmatched. [www.jamiecollinsphotography.com] Michelle Leone, my hairstylist, and Charene, my makeup artist, who made me the diva I am on the cover! [www.charene.com] Christine Grace—it's a miracle the way you breathed life into the project and pulled it all together.

My interior book designer, Howard Roberts, for being a joy to work with while bringing unique individuality to this manuscript. [www.hrobertsdesign.com]

My marketing team, Judy Klym and Crystal Slattery. I don't even know where to begin, but without the two of you, I wouldn't have made it past first base!

My writer's group—Anne, Jane, Lisa, Maryse, and Mary. Thanks for reading every draft and for finding a way to slip in encouragement along with honest opinions.

All my friends back home in Texas—you know who you are. Thank you for loving Tommy and supporting me in this next stage of my life.

My Texas family for loving me and allowing me to live my dreams.

My amazing children, Kaden, Anistyn, and Ashtyn. You three are more than any parent could ask for. Thanks for putting up with me over the last two years!

Finally, my loving husband, Rick. You have taken the term help-mate to an entirely new level. You are so much more than I ever dreamed of in a partner. I would never have been able to do this without you. Here's your one-size-fits-all white t-shirt. I love you.

Kerie Boshka
December 2010

Contents

Chapter Five: Faith

Acquiring faith and using it to your utmost advantage.

87

Chapter Six: Struggles

Learning to persist when circumstances don't go as planned.

107

Chapter Seven: Relationships

Being mindful of the way you view yourself, your surroundings, and others.

125

Chapter Eight: Blessings

Embracing change, rather than fearing it, as you begin to see God's hand at work in pulling together your life.

167

Chapter Nine: Living

Starting to live a life of happiness and abundance while giving the gifts of love and joy back to others.

191

Introduction

"Our most tragic experiences bring forth what we allow them to. There is a way to become one of those rare individuals who seems to come out of even the toughest of circumstances stronger than before. It begins by believing in yourself."

Kerie Boshka

*S*even years ago, my husband committed suicide, leaving me, my six-year-old son, and seven-week-old daughter abandoned and alone. It would be an understatement to say that, after my husband's death, I was very lost and depressed. In searching for help, I discovered that the biggest obstacle was finding someone who could relate to what I was going through. Healing finally came as I began to look for answers within myself. Ultimately, I did attain happiness and success despite the turmoil surrounding my life.

This is what led to the creation of this book. I use that experience to exemplify how I was able to allow my previous dormant faith in God to open the doors that helped me overcome unimaginable grief—and achieve happiness along the way.

You, the reader, will not only find encouragement in these pages, but you will clearly see how to open up your own life to the same amazing possibilities as I did. I will show you how to hear God for yourself. I will leave you with practical tools to help fight negativity and strengthen relationships. I will encourage you as you learn how to heal from sorrow, put an end to daily struggles, and live a life of blessing and abundance.

In spite of the desperate circumstances that might be plaguing your life, you'll find that this book will help you to gain courage and hope in the future. The material touches on many areas such as starting over, finding hope, surrendering to circumstances out of our control, resolving addictive relationships, overcoming grief, and recovering from the death of a loved one. The content is presented in a conversational, straightforward voice—making this a light and easy read—and is not limited to a specific gender, age group, or religious preference.

After the suicide of my husband, I moved to New York with nothing but two small children and faith that I was making the right choice. I overcame unimaginable odds to not only open my own business, but to become a spiritual teacher, freelance writer, and book author as well. I know from experience what you are going through and can give you a solid, practical plan to help you improve your circumstances.

This book was birthed from a place of much sorrow and deep despair. It proves that our darkest moments can be our greatest treasures. Our most tragic experiences bring forth within us truth, wisdom, and growth if we will allow them to.

Let my story and my searching help to shine light on your path. We all need love. We all need healing. We all need joy and comfort. I pray that I can somehow be a tool to help you find these riches for yourself.

Thank you for letting me be a part of your journey.

Kerie Boshka
Stamford, CT
November 2010

Chapter One

SEARCHING

"The truth is that our finest moments are most likely to occur when we are feeling deeply uncomfortable, unhappy, or unfulfilled. For it is only in such moments, propelled by our discomfort, that we are likely to step out of our ruts and start searching for different ways or truer answers."

M. Scott Peck

The First Steps

*"A tree that fills a man's embrace grows from a seed-
ling. A tower nine stories high starts with one brick.
A journey of a thousand miles begins with a single step."*
Lao Tsu

I sat quietly trying to come to terms with the shocking revelations that had recently surfaced about my family. Paralyzed with emotion, I was completely unable to
wrap my thoughts around the fact my life was beginning
to spin out of control. How could my husband betray me
in such a way?

A knock at the door offered relief as I stood to see my
father waiting for me outside. I instantly ran into the arms of
the one man who always managed to keep me safe. All I
wanted was to rest in his secure embrace, just as I had during those sheltered years of my youth. Unfortunately, today
my father would carry the burden of delivering heartbreak-
ing information to his little girl. Today he could not offer me
shelter. As the words he had come to say began to flow, I
realized this was the day my world would fall apart.

"Honey, Tommy's gone."

"What do you mean Tommy's gone—where is he?"

"He's gone, honey—Tommy is dead. He killed
himself last night."

"No, no, we just had a baby—and we have a son. He wouldn't do that to them, he wouldn't do that to me. No, you're wrong!"

My dad proceeded to say my husband's body was found a few hours before in Fort Worth. The car was still running when the police pulled out his body… The next thing I remember was being picked up off the floor and helped onto the bed. I was shaking uncontrollably and overcome by disbelief and terror as I felt myself die inside.

My daughter, Anistyn, was seven weeks old. My son, Kaden, would be turning seven in twelve days. I had instantly become a twenty-eight-year-old widow. Not only had I recently discovered my entire marriage had been a lie, but now I would never know the whole truth. The only person able to reveal the facts to me had chosen to leave me for good. I would never plead my case or scream at my husband for what he had done. I would never be able to tell him I knew his secrets and hear his response. The end of our road had come. I would never see him again.

My life hadn't always been this unstable. Tommy and I grew up in a quaint Texas town just outside of Fort Worth. Aledo wasn't simply a small town. It was an amazing group of people who fit together like family. Kids could safely ride dirt bikes through the streets. It was common to see a cowboy taking his horse in place of a car. There was a town newspaper, but the announcements people were most interested in reading were the ones painted on the building next to the train tracks. If a new baby was born or someone wanted to profess their love, it would be announced on the side of the building. Football games were the highlight of the week. The entire town would close down to watch their beloved Bearcats in action. We all grew up together under those bright Friday night lights, warming ourselves under layers of clothes and blankets, sipping hot chocolate, and eating Frito pie.

I was fresh into high school when I met my future husband. He was mysterious, good-looking, fun, and the ever popular star running back. Tommy Bouldin was also the high school bad boy who always seemed to find a path to trouble. The fact that he was everything I had been warned to avoid, never really mattered. His charm, good looks, crowd-pleasing mannerisms, and ability to make every day an adventure hooked me from the start. Tommy had a way of getting what he wanted. I was all too happy to be included on his list of desires.

I, on the other hand, had always played it safe. I grew up in a very strict Christian home—where rules were made to be followed, where there was little room for mistakes, and even less for rebellion, where disobedience brought severe consequences. To my parents' distress, having a good time was my new boyfriend's number one priority. Being a part of his life meant finding a way to work around my family's strict guidelines. I quickly set aside my morals and began drinking and hanging out with Tommy's group of friends. I naively followed any road that would take me straight to him. I abandoned all too much of my true self to be the person I thought would make Tommy happy.

I had always been a leader who stood up for her individual values. Now, I had become a follower with little voice of my own. I soon learned that relationships are never easy when one person has to give entirely of herself to make things work. Nonetheless, I became convinced no price was too high if the result was keeping Tommy in my life. We would fight. He would leave. I would do whatever was necessary to get him back. Tommy didn't compromise. He wanted things to go his way. As foolish as it sounds, my fear of losing him was worse than the pain I experienced holding on. In the end, I found myself willing to alter my persona in many damaging ways to avoid making unnecessary waves.

After an on-again-off-again courtship, Tommy and I became parents at twenty and were married at twenty-one. To no one's surprise, our marriage didn't turn out to be the fairy tale of my dreams. Violent fights, arguments, hours of crying, and me sleeping with the baby in my arms seemed to be the way in our home. From day one and continuing throughout our marriage, my husband would walk out if things became too difficult. Each time this happened, I would win him back by giving in and letting him have his way. I naively remained hopeful that someday our relationship would miraculously change for the better.

After six years of marriage, my husband came clean. He had been hiding a secret life with cocaine. He sold drugs, took money, lied to friends and family, and would go to whatever means necessary to support his addiction. Surprisingly, I was caught off guard by his confession. It was a relief to finally understand where the disappearances, unprovoked mood swings, and eva-sive behavior had come from. But this knowledge did nothing to shed light on why I had been willing to put up with this lifestyle.

I was the one who did whatever it took to enable this relationship to continue. I was the one foolish enough to mistake misery as happiness. I was the one who chose to stay. The harsh reality became clear. My life would never improve, even if my husband was will-ing to work on his faults, if I was unwilling to come clean myself. Tommy's changes alone would never bring me true happiness. Lasting joy was something I would only find within myself.

It was obvious that my past actions of denial and control would never produce a meaningful lifestyle. I had rejected the call of my own heart in hopes of pleas-ing others for much too long. My anger and frustration quickly turned to depression, and I soon became des-perate to end the agony.

The grief and loneliness I carried for years lifted as I began to plead with God for help. Once I was able to express my true feelings, peace began to take over. I'd heard the teacher would appear when the student was ready. Without question, my reaching a point where I was willing to listen allowed me to finally hear from my Guide.

I read Ezekiel 36:27: *And I will put my spirit in you, <u>causing</u> you to be guided by my rules, and you will keep my orders and do them* (Emphasis added). This is where my journey to happiness began. This verse held the key to my finding peace. The only way to follow God's rules was to be guided by His Spirit. I had been trusting in my physical body to lead me to a place where only the Spirit was equipped to take me. My unhappiness and confusion had been a result of my attempting to control the chaos around me and within me.

The more I reflected on my life and this new revelation, the more I could see the truth. My depression was not God's punishment. He was simply waiting for me to allow Him to lead me out of my hopelessness. I could feel a Presence, assuring me it was time to rest and trust God. Regardless of what state my life was in, God had continued to love me unconditionally.

I wasn't sure I could fully trust in the simplicity of the wisdom I had discovered...*don't fix the problem; just rest.* While this didn't make sense to my logical way of thinking, I knew somehow it was truth.

I had always believed that God lived inside of me. Growing up, I attended church so often it felt like a second home. Sadly, until now I had never experienced the ease and comfort that came from placing God in charge. I was finally beginning to see the bigger picture. Salvation wasn't simply a prayer I said to purchase a ticket out of hell. Nor was it something I had to pay for every day through righteous acts. My salvation was a gift of service given to me by a loving Father who was willing to live His life through me and carry my burdens and struggles for me. God did this by placing within me His Spirit, a Spirit capable of leading me out of any storm. The only requirement was to surrender my old ways and learn how to follow my Spirit's guidance.

If I truly believed God dwelt inside of me, I also had to acknowledge that His perfection did as well. There was no doubt God had a funny way of showing His perfection. With my violent temper, lack of self control, and marriage to an addict, my life didn't resemble any place where God would desire to live. In any case, I knew my world had instantly changed by the discovery of this one simple principle: the way to gaining the peace my heart longed for was to let go and allow God to express His perfect nature through me.

I began to see God was living inside of my husband as well. In a sense, I was married to God. God was living in me; this meant God loved my husband through me. **GOD WAS IN IT ALL AND WAS DOING IT ALL.** If God was doing the work through us, there was no way we could fail. I was able to trust that my child and I were living in a safe environment, despite the circumstances surrounding our lives, because I had allowed God to be in complete control. Given this knowledge, I was able to experience peace.

I couldn't believe the freeing power this new revelation brought to my life. Tommy was no longer my problem. Now was the time for me to stop attempting to fix my husband and give him over to his own Spirit. It was time I let go. I couldn't imagine things getting any worse. God couldn't possibly screw up my life any more than I had. I honestly thought I had nothing to lose.

I brought Tommy home from the rehabilitation clinic with a fresh outlook on myself and him. I believed that my prayers over my husband had been answered.

Despite the fact that Tommy was anything but spotless, I knew in my heart that he was exactly where God intended for him to be.

For the first time, I no longer saw God as a mere righteous, superior figure. God had become my companion. Every day opened a new doorway to spiritual enlightenment and happiness. My husband was amazed that I was no longer brought down by the same arguments that had plagued us in the past. I had no reason to fight for Tommy's love and acceptance because I no longer considered him to be the source from which I received those things. I had no need to fight for a commitment I could never lose.

I never doubted God was in control. No matter what circumstance the moment brought, I believed God would work everything out. Romans 8:28 would continue to play over and over in my head…*we know that all things work together for good for those who love God, to those who are called according to his purpose.* Obstacles were no longer something to dread, but to honor. **My struggles were perfecting me and bringing me to the life of peace and harmony I had sought for so many years.**

Little by little our lives began to improve. For starters, we were finally able to purchase our first home. Tommy didn't change his old patterns overnight, but he began to show genuine concern for my needs and desires. His choices began to revolve more around our family and less around himself. He involved himself not only in our son's life, but in mine as well. He would take me to lunch in the afternoon, cook me dinner in the evening, and rub my back until I fell asleep at night. I even remember him sitting down to watch a few romantic comedies. I felt secure in who my husband was because I totally trusted in the perfection of Spirit. I finally found hope and believed this hope would never disappoint me.

Two years later, just after the birth of our second child, the high I believed would never end began to crumble. I received a phone call from my mother informing me that Tommy had been caught on tape taking money from our family business. The words I heard from the other end of the receiver were the kind that throw your life into an uncontrollable spiral. Tommy appeared to have made so many positive changes. I was devastated to learn that he had reverted back to his old ways.

I could barely digest the news I had just been given. I sat paralyzed on the bathroom floor, yet shaking uncontrollably. My head was spinning, and my heart was racing. I was frantically trying to get a grip on myself. I felt betrayed and terribly abandoned. How could this have happened? How could Tommy be willing to sacrifice everything we had for his selfish gratification once again?

My family confronted my husband by phone, and though he denied the charges, he gave up the fight once he was informed he had been caught on tape. After their conversation, my mom told me there had been a long pause from my husband once he found out I had been informed of the situation. He then said he needed to take a little time to sort things out and would discuss the matter with us later that evening.

My heart was crushed, and my dreams were shattered. In spite of my circumstances, my main concern was to remain strong and to give my children the structure and safe environment they deserved. I convinced myself I could manage my emotions under the disappointment and pressure. I would repeat to myself over and over again: *God, You are in control. I will not look at this storm as ultimate. You are in control and You will guide me through this. God, You are in control.*

The devastating call—revealing that Tommy was stealing from my parents—came on Friday morning. I somehow managed to keep my calm until Sunday night. It had been almost three days since I had spoken to Tommy. He had a habit of running from issues, so it wasn't a surprise that I hadn't heard from him. But his close friends hadn't heard from him either, and that wasn't typical. I was sure he would have been in touch with one of them by now. I had to find out where he had gone. I began the search for answers.

I desperately needed to exercise some form of power and learn the truth once and for all. I went onto Tommy's computer to see if I could find clues as to where he might be. By chance, my husband had received an e-mail giving the profile password he requested for a particular adult website he frequented. It turned out drugs weren't Tommy's only addiction. I may not have come any closer to finding out where my husband was, but it was now obvious where he had been!

My eyes were fixed on the validation that my husband lived many different lives. I had uncovered evidence proving the past thirteen years of my life had been a complete lie. Neither my marriage or my husband was what I thought they were. I had no idea what was real. It was obvious Tommy had been hiding his drug addiction from me with the money he took from my family. But the e-mail revealed a much bigger story. My husband had been pursuing relationships with other women and couples by contacting them online. On top of everything else, Tommy was a sex addict.

"Discretion is a must" would read as the headline of his e-mail communications with them. He had been meeting strangers during the day in a hotel room that he had gained access to at any time. As the outside customer service representative for my family's business, he had been able to easily meet with these people on a regular basis by leaving work to "check on jobs." This gave him an opportunity to disappear without raising too many red flags. The evidence was clear. There was no denying what had been occurring throughout our marriage.

I fell asleep Sunday night only to wake in an absolute panic. I had a sick feeling something was terribly wrong. I was terrified and found myself pleading to God. The only emotion I could describe would be a desperate appeal…*please, don't let grace run out, don't let Your grace run out, don't let Your grace run out.* I couldn't let go of this inward cry flowing from my heart. I couldn't stop begging God to save Tommy. I had no idea why I would pray for such a thing. Tommy might be hiding out somewhere, but everyone knew how much Tommy loved Tommy. He would do things to hurt other people, but he would never hurt himself. I had no real clue as to why I had become so hysterical or why I would even care for God to help him at this point. Something inside of me simply would not let go.

Despite these new revelations, I still loved my husband very much. I could see the kindness and love he had to give, the extraordinary man he was capable of becoming. I wished with all of my heart that he could believe in himself and love himself as much as I did. Tommy continually ran from life, trying to find the missing pieces through drugs, sex, alcohol, and material objects. He had been unable to see that this only left him more lost and miserable. I wanted him to let go and trust his heart so he could gain self-respect and finally experience peace, but he had to make the choice himself.

It was hard to believe the sharp turns that my life had so unexpectedly taken. On Friday morning, I woke up to a playful argument with Tommy about dog slobber on the bed. By Sunday evening I discovered my husband, my marriage, my life, and possibly my future were never what I had thought they were.

Now, standing here at my front door, feeling as if life could not possibly get any worse, I received yet another blow. One sentence from my father would deliver the new reality in which I was now forced to accept. How could everything go so wrong, so fast? How could a life that took years to build come crashing to an end with the sound of a few simple words?

The fact that God would let me see so much hope in the future and then allow it to be taken in such a devastating way left me completely defeated. I surrendered my most valuable possession, my family, to Him, and He did nothing to stop it from breaking beyond repair. How could a loving God have consented to this? I didn't believe God caused Tommy to kill himself, but He did have the power to prevent it. If He loved me, why had He not stopped this? I trusted Him with everything, only to find my entire world shattered beyond repair.

Betrayal

"To love is to risk not being loved in return. To hope is to risk pain. To try is to risk failure, but risk must be taken, because the greatest hazard in life is to risk nothing."

Anonymous

I was immediately thrown into the whirlwind; grieving the loss of my husband, planning his funeral, breaking the news of Tommy's death to dear friends and family, supporting my children, and dealing with new revelations from the past. Each one of these tasks was overwhelming. I didn't know where to start or how to begin. Life was hopeless. Tommy's suicide made it impossible to mend these bridges. He was gone and would never come home. Somehow my body managed to switch into autopilot. I was hurled full force into forward motion whether I wanted to or not. How was I to tell my son that his father was dead?

My sister went to pick Kaden up from school and bring him home to me. I was about to take a six-year-old child out of his familiar world of fun, play, colors, friends, and imagination to force him into a new reality of abandonment, heartache, and confusion. How could a mother do that to her child? How could I not have protected him? How could I have failed so miserably at providing him with the stability children need from their parents? How was he going to survive something I myself didn't have the strength to survive? I was afraid of losing the carefree child I had grown so purely in love with. To look at my little boy as he walked in the door and know I was about to break his fragile heart into tiny pieces almost killed me.

I worked with everything I had to be strong for Kaden as I walked with him into his room. My son had just been abandoned by one parent. I refused to have him question my loyalty. I felt the only way to provide him with any kind of stability was through honesty. Too many lies had been told in our home. I refused to tell another one.

He asked me what was wrong, and I told him we had to talk about Daddy. I told him Daddy wasn't coming home. I felt Kaden needed to know the truth in order to fully recover, but how would I be honest about suicide with a six-year-old child? Finally, I told him that Daddy had been very sick—that he went to Fort Worth and fell asleep in his car and had gone to heaven to be with God. I could see his mind trying to piece together the words I had spoken. He simply asked, "Mommy, is Daddy dead?" I could only reply by saying "yes." We sat on the bed and cried together until Kaden asked me to leave so he could be alone.

Nothing could help me comprehend how a faithful and loving God would allow this much pain and suffering into my life and the lives of so many innocent others. But somehow my spiritual-self was able to comfort me. I knew that I had begun a journey down a road to spiritual maturity. No matter how bad the situation looked at the moment, or how victimized I felt, I knew God had not forsaken me.

I cried with all of my heart for God to keep me afloat during this misery. I prayed that somehow Tommy's life would miraculously touch others in a positive way and that God would allow goodness to arise from the ashes of this disaster. The same words would continually run through my mind over and over again *...all things work for good, all things work for good, all things work for good.*

I pleaded for guidance.

"Please, God, walk me by your Spirit. Guide my words, guide my steps, and give me the grace to honor You by honoring Tommy. I need You. Don't let me lose faith because I can't see through the clouds! I love You. No matter what my circumstance brings, please help me see that You are and always will be faithful. Please help me walk by Your Spirit. Please protect me from myself. Protect me from anger and bitterness. Help me to see Tommy the way You see him. Your ways are not our ways. Lord, I beg You to help me walk in Your ways. Please don't let me doubt my relationship with You because of my disappointment. Help me Lord, God, help me. You remain in control. I will trust you even through the destruction of my life."

Amen.

I had one final sacrifice to give my marriage, my husband's funeral. In spite of my anger and confusion, I wanted to say my last good-bye with love and respect. I wanted to honor Tommy. I wanted to bury him with the dignity his death appeared to have taken away. I wanted people to see the best of how Tommy lived and not the way he died. I wanted to let my children know they were not to blame and should never feel ashamed. There was so much I wanted to accomplish, yet I didn't know if I would have the strength to get out of bed. I knew my desires were God's desires flowing through me and, therefore, I could trust that God's grace would be sufficient for me. *God's strength was made perfect in my weakness* (2 Corinthians 12:9). That's what I needed, perfect strength.

I flew to Dallas where my husband's lifeless body awaited me. As I arrived at the police station, an officer asked to speak with me privately. He told me that he had been the one to respond to the call and was there when the ambulance retrieved my husband's body. In his years with the force, he had never come across someone more tenacious about completing the task at hand. On Friday afternoon, Tommy had driven three hundred miles from Lubbock to Fort Worth, found a quiet field, run an automotive hose from the tailpipe to the inside of his vehicle, taped the windows and doors closed so little poison would be able to escape, and ended his life. He must have had a full tank of gas because it appeared he had been dead for hours. Monday morning would be the reported time of death. However, he likely committed suicide late Sunday night.

Days later, when I arrived at the funeral home, I was escorted to a private viewing room where at last my husband and I would be together. He was wearing the brown turtleneck sweater and denim blue jeans he had worn for our family pictures taken just days before he disappeared. I could see him and touch him, but I could not be with him. My heart screamed out in desperation. I cried and pleaded with him to come back. There was no answer. He wasn't there.

I stared at a cold shell of the man I dreamed of loving for the rest of my life. His hands were the only part still resembling the man he had been less than a week before. I held them while bowing my head on his motionless chest. He would not have wanted to be here. He wouldn't have wanted me or anyone to see him like this. Still, I had to say goodbye. I needed to see his body one last time to convince myself he wasn't coming home.

I begged God to give him back to me. I begged for relief. As unhealthy as this part of my life had been, I pleaded with God not to allow it to be taken away. In spite of my cries for help, I would be forced to bury my old life and continue forward without my family intact. I didn't want it this way! I wanted a future with my family and this husband. I wanted to go back, but I couldn't. The way to my heart's desires would be ahead of me. I had no choice but to move forward and say goodbye. I was being forced to leave Tommy behind.

Later that evening at the viewing, I walked Kaden over to the table where we had placed his father's pictures and albums. I asked him to be in charge of putting the pictures around so people could remember Daddy the way we did. He immediately responded, arranging and rearranging pictures, telling story after story of each one. "This is where he yelled at me because I didn't run fast enough at my soccer game. This is when I almost got sick because he buried me in so much snow. I want to be a football player just like Daddy when I grow up." My heart was coming out of my chest as I rehashed these stories with Kaden, but I consistently felt the loyalty of my Spirit pulling me through with intensity, helping me guide my son away from total despair with strength and wisdom.

We said goodbye to Tommy on a flawless December day. The sun comforted us with the warmth and beauty of its light. The ceremony overlooked a peaceful fountain, and a wall of roses miraculously remaining in bloom. I was escorted in, standing next to my son and carrying a baby wrapped in a white blanket and delicate matching dress. Kaden was feeling very proud in his first suit and tie, carrying his Daddy's favorite football.

I met my mother-in-law for the first time that day. Over the years, I had witnessed Tommy agonize over her abandonment of him. Now here she was, standing before me and his children, ready to once again say goodbye to her child. We had located her a few years earlier in hopes of building a relationship. Unfortunately, little became of our efforts. Who meets her husband's mother at his funeral? To me she was simply the person at the top of a long line of disappointments my husband faced on a daily basis.

I prepared a statement I wanted to share with the guests. My devoted cousin reluctantly but willingly shared my thoughts for me:

I want to thank all of you for coming, for loving my husband, and to tell all of you how sorry I am for your loss.

God tells us He won't give us more than we can handle. That doesn't mean there will never be a circumstance too much for us to bear. It is in these situations that God loves us enough to pick us up and carry us through them.

I also know it's not our actions that define who we are because we all make mistakes. Our heart is what defines us. Our heart is what God sees. Tommy's heart was precious, tender, and filled with love for all of you. We can't love people in pieces. If we love them, then we love all of them.

My last gift to you, Tommy, is that I will continue to love and adore you unconditionally for the rest of my life. I will see you every day in the lives of your beautiful children. I will honor you, and I will be strong for them.

Tommy didn't take this path for lack of love. He did love us all so much. Always remember that love, how much Tommy enjoyed life, and how precious he truly was.

Kerie

After collecting my husband's ashes, I took him back to the place where he had surrendered his life. Meditating there helped me begin to make peace with the current situation. Here I was able to let go of much of my anger. I couldn't imagine the desperation and pain my husband must have felt while sitting in this very place. I couldn't comprehend the kind of mental torture he must have felt to accept death as the only form of relief. It must have been unimaginable to be buried so deep inside a tortured mind that dying would seem the only way out. I knew it wouldn't be fair for me to judge him for making foolish choices behind an unhealthy logic I was incapable of understanding. Coming to terms with this helped me begin to find forgiveness.

During the drive back to Lubbock, all of the joyful memories of the past came rushing back as I pondered our life together. It seemed impossible to go on with such a huge part of me missing. Who would I become? Could there possibly be hope for my life after this? There was nothing I could do to stop myself from moving forward toward a destination I didn't want to reach. I was on my way to a new beginning, a new world, and a new me.

This is where my story begins. This was my starting point to truly recognizing that life is good and that happiness is attainable despite one's circumstances. It was not always easy, and the process took time, but eventually I became more and more in touch with the Spirit dwelling inside of me. I learned how sometimes our greatest challenges can also become our biggest blessings. By sharing the healing wisdom I received through the havoc of my life, it is my hope that you, too, will be able to find victory over your circumstances and achieve unconditional happiness as well. May God bless and speak to you on this journey.

"The world is round, and the place which may seem like the end may also be the beginning."
Ivy Baker Priest

Chapter Two

SORROW

*"Sorrow is properly that state of the mind
in which our desires are fixed upon the past,
without looking forward to the future, an
incessant wish that something were otherwise
than it has been, and a tormenting and harass-
ing want of some enjoyment or possession
which we have lost, and which no endeavors
can possibly regain. Into such anguish many
have sunk upon some sudden diminution of
their fortune, an unexpected blast of their
reputation, or the loss of children or of friends.
They have suffered all sensibility of pleasure
to be destroyed by a single blow, have given
up forever the hopes of substituting any other*

object in the room for that which they lament, resigned their lives to gloom and despondency, and worn themselves out in unfailing misery."

Samuel Johnson

Finding Hope

"Until this moment, I never understood how hard it was to lose something you never had."

Anonymous

I arrived home desperately afraid of the new life awaiting me. The walls that were once a safe and reassuring refuge were now the breeding ground for despair. Tommy's belongings remained to deceive my mind into thinking my husband could once again come through the door. The dog even sat by the window waiting for his favorite companion's arrival.

Reality overwhelmed me as I realized the magnitude of my despair. The house seemed so familiar, yet the most familiar part of my life was gone forever. Hopelessness began to suffocate me. I wanted to trust God, I wanted Him to save me, but how could I ever put what little I had left back into His hands? My Spirit's strength had pulled me through thus far, but I was afraid that if I gave God further control, He might allow more to be taken away. I had lost all sense of security and could bear no more heartache. I longed to be cared for during this fragile state of mourning, but I was also terrified of what this vulnerability could do to me.

My heart remained in a past built on illusions. The memories I relied on to bring me comfort were memories of deception. I knew only what my husband allowed me to see. The reality that I would never fully know the truth haunted me. Even my family believed the facts of Tommy's indiscretions needed to be kept hidden. They may have been trying to shield me from pain, but I should have been told the truth. Their misguided protection stripped away my power and deprived me of the chance to stop the spiral of destruction.

Everyone I knew allowed me to live in a lie. As I began to observe people and see what they were capable of, I realized I would never fully understand anyone's motives. Secrets have the power to destroy lives. Unfortunately, everyone has secrets.

Time continued to move forward, but I saw nothing to believe in. I was unable to find comfort in a world where uncertainty, truth, and safety were never guaranteed. Each minute brought a heavier dose of suspicion, grief, and fear. My body began to buckle under the pressure. I no longer wanted to live. The thoughts that brought peace were the thoughts of how easily this could all end. I could take my life. I could leave the miserable place I had been forced to live in and terminate this grief once and for all.

Strangely, these were the thoughts that brought me hope—until, that is, I remembered my two precious children. Memories flooded me of those big blue eyes looking up to me for strength and guidance, the tiny hands only wanting to hold mine, the innocent hearts beating because of my desire to have them near. My children needed to see hope in this world. They needed reassurance that good does exist. It was vital that they have an example to follow, and I was the only one who could provide it. They would have no need to search for truth and stability elsewhere if they could see it at home in their mother. I resolved that I would give them my all to protect them from further suffering. My children's happiness was worth fighting for. I had no choice but to find a way to make my new life count—if not for me, for them.

Moving On

"When you feel that you have reached the end and that you cannot go one step further, when life seems to be drained of all purpose: What a wonderful opportunity to start all over again, to turn over a new page."

Eileen Caddy

Christmas arrived five days after my husband's funeral—Anistyn's first Christmas and Kaden's first big event without his father. I was determined to somehow enjoy the holidays as a family. I wanted my children to carry good memories from this day forward. I resolved myself to battle the rush of last-minute Christmas shoppers.

I became immobilized by sorrow once I arrived home from shopping. How would I label the gifts? Would they be from Mom and Dad, or just Mom? Which would be less depressing: to remind everyone of the father who couldn't make it home to celebrate with his children, or to shut him out of the picture altogether? I decided to print both of our names on the few gifts Tommy had planned to buy, tossed the remaining unmarked presents into boxes, and drove toward my parent's house.

My family gathered together the way we do every year, but this year we were trying harder than usual to maintain the appearance of a happy home. We opened presents, sat down for the typical Christmas meal, played with Kaden's new toys, and took turns holding the baby.

Nonetheless, the joy and purpose of the occasion were missing. Tommy's absence overpowered the room. He always had a fierce presence about him. His absence was even stronger. His betrayal had affected us all differently, but despite our tarnished memories of the past, our love for him would never cease. This was the moment I realized that living may very well be the most painful thing I would ever have to do.

Surprisingly, Kaden's load seemed to lighten a bit. For a time, he was like his old self. He actually wanted to be with me. What little I had left to give was enough for him. He found comfort and hope in being together with my family and watching me try to move forward. I realized that the best action I could possibly take for my son was to be a part of his life. I didn't have to be the hero. I simply had to show my children how much they were loved.

I stayed with my family until I found myself starting to be consumed with grief once again. I left Kaden and Anistyn with their grandparents so I could return home and retreat to the solitude of my bedroom. This was the only place I felt I could let it all go. Here, I didn't have to pretend to be strong. I didn't have to speak to anyone. I was free to be whatever I needed to be. I could drop into bed and completely fall apart.

I believed in God and was aware of my Spirit, but I didn't quite know what to do with them. I was trying to do what was right for my family, but I had no idea how to begin a healing process and little strength left to try. I prayed, but mostly cried. I didn't know how I would meet the demands the future required of me. Going to work, paying bills, and caring for two small children were simple tasks any normal parent should be able to perform with ease. I couldn't find the strength.

The only way I knew to press ahead was to take one tiny step at a time. If I was going to live again, I could not allow the important moments of my life to pass me by. I had to stop dwelling on the past, quit fearing the future, and begin to make the best possible decisions for the moment. The hurdle I now faced was finding the strength to keep going. I found that by simply moving. Finding hope in today's blessings was the way I began to look at each situation.

I allowed myself to be grateful that I would forever witness Tommy living on through our children. I could see his laugh and lighthearted personality coming alive in Kaden, his contagious smile and sensitivity coming through in Anistyn. They were given the best of their father. Witnessing my children's laughter and being able to see pieces of my husband through their actions helped me find joy.

Meeting the needs of these two amazing people became my focus. I was able to find the strength to provide for them physically, but helping them heal from their emotional scars was another story. I could never guarantee their safety because I no longer believed in it. I could not offer them comfort because I no longer felt it. To fulfill my parental duty, I had to find a way to call upon qualities I no longer possessed. The only way to keep from panic was to go back to lesson one: My children and I were in a safe environment, despite the chaos taking place around us, because God was in control and He would not let me fail. I would have all I needed by leaning on Him.

In spite of my decision to put my hope in God, I watched in frustration as things continued to go downhill. I couldn't do anything without Him, and, with Him, nothing seemed to go right either. My eyes could see what needed to be done. My head could figure out the actions necessary to improve our situation, but my mind simply immobilized my body from taking action.

Kaden began living in absolute fear. He was tormented by the idea that parents would abandon their children if life became too difficult. He was afraid my heartache would take me away. To him, my broken heart was a much bigger concern than his own. He innocently covered up his panic to take care of his mother.

He was on the road to following in his father's footsteps by dealing with problems by guarding himself with a shield of avoidance. My only way of protecting my child was to show him that hiding would never solve problems. Confronting misfortune is the only way to overcome it. Only by my example would Kaden learn how to heal.

To start, I had to let him see me accept my own brokenness. It was my hope that, by doing this, I would help him feel comfortable enough to do the same. In addition, I had to stop concealing my heartache behind a false wall of courage. The only way I could give my son security was by not offering him a false sense of it. I had to teach him that my hurt was a natural part of the healing process.

I decided to trust my intuition and give Kaden the facts about his father's suicide. My mind could not comprehend that adding trauma to an already fragile child would be a positive decision. Yet, the more I prayed and asked God for guidance, the more certain I became that this was the right action to take.

I read somewhere that the one major regret in children who had survived the suicide of a parent is that they had not been told the truth up front. Once the facts eventually surface, surviving children are forced to revisit their grief and loss all over again. In turn, they begin to doubt the living parent's motives as well. I would not allow my lack of honesty to hinder my son's growth or cause division later on. I would never allow Kaden to suffer this kind of pain a second time.

Kaden was upset and confused by my confession, but I could see his relief. His fear of losing me instantly began to fade. My trusting Kaden helped him put his trust back in me. I admitted to him that I did not have all of the answers. I told him I would be sad most of the time. I assured him it was okay to cry and fall apart. I let him know I would do my best, but I would not be perfect. I said the one thing I knew for certain was that I loved him unconditionally. I would never intentionally leave or hurt him. We would figure out a way of dealing with our heartache and disappointment together. Somehow, in spite of his fear of abandonment, he was able to once again lean on me for support.

Protection

"Every man has his secret sorrows which the world knows not; and often times we call a man cold when he is only sad."

Henry Wadsworth Longfellow

I didn't know who I was any more. I began to wonder if I ever really knew myself. Emptiness consumed me. There was nothing left of me to offer. Nobody knew how to handle me. Not a single person could figure out how to meet my needs. I was simply a fragile piece of glass full of nicks and cracks. One wrong word, and I would shatter. I was no longer the same carefree person I had been in the past. People would try to encourage me by telling me things would get better, but no one truly understood my emptiness.

Secrets and lies continued to come out into the open to further bury me in my despair. I felt more and more betrayed as people came clean with information about Tommy's life. As more proof of his betrayal surfaced, I began to blame everyone around me for my husband's death. I blamed his drug dealer for allowing him to use. I blamed my family for hiding the truth of Tommy's many indiscretions. I blamed my husband's friends for helping him conceal his lies. Most of all, I blamed myself for being so blind. My life was consumed with blame.

Out of fear, I began to withdraw from everyone around me. In my mind I could not allow anyone to damage me further. The only way I knew of protecting myself was to build heavy walls around my heart. I shut out the world by burying the love and compassion I naturally felt for people.

I had no patience for anyone or anything. I would attack whatever stood in the way of my achieving peace. Loving, in my eyes, was the door to pain. The only way to avoid that pain was to avoid love.

As much as I cared for my family and children, even they were held at arm's length. I became cold, cruel, and uncaring. My inconsistent behavior led people to approach me with caution. They had no way of knowing if their presence would provoke a screaming match or if I would revert to my cold shell and shut them out altogether. There was no rhyme or reason to my unpredictable behavior. I was unmoved by other people's pain and didn't care who was hurt by my actions.

In order to give my heart time to heal, I isolated myself. However helpful this seemed to be, a huge problem still remained. Shutting out the world was hurting me more than protecting me from others. Each dagger I let fly with my tongue sent razor-sharp debris back to my own conscience. I was ripping myself into tiny bits each passing day by my self-absorbed actions. By locking myself behind feelings of bitterness and hate, I was allowing my protective walls to crush me.

Even though my actions were separating me from everyone, deep down I hoped it would be possible to connect again. When I look back on that time, I remember searching for meaning and truth in everything and everyone. It was as if I had become desperate to find someone to trust so I could restore some form of peace.

I wasn't quite sure if I was more afraid of destroying myself through my isolation or of opening the door enough to let those around me enter. Both options left me vulnerable, and I was terrified of pain. My only means of survival was to begin to open my heart to my Spirit and once again allow myself to be guided toward life.

The Power to Change

"Heaven itself is reached with empty hands and open minds, which come with nothing to find everything and claim it as their own."

A Course in Miracles

*M*y depression and sorrow were heavy indeed. What I didn't realize was that I had placed much of the grief on myself. I had chosen to carry doubt, panic, fear, anger, and frustration. I didn't want to believe this, but as I began to examine a very simple vision that had come to me, I better understood the damage I was doing to myself.

In this vision I could see myself standing in front of a table holding two glass bowls. The bowl on the right was labeled A; the bowl on the left, B. In the middle were strips of paper and a pen. Each thought that came to my mind would immediately be written down on one of these strips. As the vision began to unfold, I was able to see the importance of holding my thoughts captive.

My first thought, a generally positive statement of direction, would be written on a strip of paper and placed in bowl A. The thoughts that followed were usually discouraging, full of doubt, reasoning, and fear; they went into bowl B.

For example, the first thought, the one from bowl A, was *pray.* The following thoughts were: *I'm too tired to pray...praying never does any good...God won't listen to me...why waste time?* They all ended up in bowl B.

My next thought, *believe in Me,* came quickly and was immediately placed in A. But negative thoughts followed again and began to fill up B: *I've tried believing and it never does any good...I can't believe something I don't see will help me...so many people say different things about You...I don't even know what to believe.*

The back and forth continued. *Give to others* went into A. *I don't have money...I'm all alone...I have nothing to give...nobody cares for me* went into B.

I had only begun, yet the uneven weight of the two bowls was obvious. Bowl A held the answers to my prayers and pointed the way to escape from my sorrow and despair. Bowl B's contents reinforced my measure of resistance.

I had been holding tight to bowl B thoughts and dwelling on fear and doubt as my lifeline. I had mistakenly believed them to be truth. I could visually see myself strain to pick up this bowl. It was full and heavier than the other, but I chose to pick it up regardless. I could feel the burden as this load was stationed onto my back. In spite of the discomfort it caused, I continued to choose to carry on and ignore the strips that awaited me in bowl A.

Bowl B contained nothing that would lead me to productive action. Not one thought inside the bowl could help me improve my situation. I had simply burdened myself by hauling around a bowl of doubt, fear, and confusion. By doing this, I had created even more negative thoughts, more doubt, and more fear. I had begun a never-ending cycle of disaster.

Another thought came for bowl A: *let it go.* Then more for bowl B: *I can't let go…I don't know how to let go…everything will fall apart if I do.*

I could feel the added pain with each passing thought. Bowl A was very light, containing only *pray… believe in Me…give to others…let it go.* These were all of the thoughts **given** to me so I might find a way to once again experience hope and see positive change take place. Bowl B held nothing but excuses. Holding on to these kept me from healing. Until I was willing to let go of bowl B, my depression and sorrow would only intensify.

As I considered this dream of letting go, I could see how my bowl B of blame and bitterness had weighed me down. I had chosen to see only the negative in people. If I looked for the good in others, I would surely find it. If I continued to look for bad, I would find it as well. It didn't take long for me to have the opportunity I needed to change my way of thinking.

Lay down your burden and begin to follow My voice immediately popped into my head, followed by my typical train of B thoughts: *how do I do that...how do I begin?* But, no, I no longer wanted to carry around burdensome baggage. I put bowl B down and chose to avoid filling it with needless thoughts.

Cry...free yourself with tears.

But I can't...I have too much that must be taken care of. No, once again I wanted to choose bowl A. I let go and allowed myself to cry. A river of tears began to flow as I let all of my fear and heartache run through me. I had put my children in their grandparent's care. I had refused to talk with family or friends. I hadn't phoned in to work. I had been in bed for three days, abandoning the responsibilities of my home, work, and children. Yet everything continued to function in spite of my absence. God had everything under control as He supernaturally cared for every area of my life. Little by little, I could feel the weight of the load I had carried begin to lift.

Go see your family.

I wasn't quite ready to leave the solitude of my bedroom, but I vowed to follow my first thought of positive direction without hesitation. My family had definitely been worried, but they had known I needed time to myself. Kaden was very happy to see me. Our little separation had given him a break from watching his mother fight to keep it together. This did wonders for his confidence. My willingness to let go had begun to make room for healing to occur. I held my daughter and played with my son. My children and I had our first good day since Tommy died.

We went home together, where I vowed to stay in touch with my thoughts of positive direction. They were my lifeline to survival.

Turn off the television and clean the house. No problem. Just as I put the kids to bed and prepared myself to collapse, another thought came to mind: *Put the pictures of Tommy back on the walls.*

I had taken the pictures to Dallas for Tommy's memorial service, but had been emotionally unable to look at them since. Coming home to the smell of his cologne, his clothes hanging in my closet, even his toothbrush sitting on the sink were already too much for me to handle. Now I was thinking of piling on more reminders of my loss. Yes! I had to be faithful to my positive pursuits even through difficult decisions if I was going to succeed. After wasting effort on useless reasoning, I gave up and hung the pictures.

The next morning I realized it was time to begin making decisions about my future. Tommy's death occurred on the day I had been scheduled to return to work from maternity leave. I had yet to deal with going back. My first thought immediately was *quit this job and go to work for your family.* I resisted the idea for many typical B reasons: *I didn't want to depend on my family to support me...I felt terrible leaving my job after they had graciously provided me with so much time off...I worried about money.* All of these thoughts were only going to complicate my life. I finally let them go and resigned from my job.

I was worried about letting people down, but making the decision to leave gave me the freedom I needed to make my children, the two people I absolutely couldn't disappoint, my first priority. In the long run, this turned out to be the best choice I could have possibly made.

With each new day, I became more and more comfortable with following this positive path. As I did, the pieces of my life began to build together toward a productive purpose. The length of my healing was all a matter of choice. God had given me wisdom along with free will. I had to choose wisdom or continue to suffer in self-imposed grief. There was a way out. I simply had to be willing to choose it.

"History, despite its wrenching pain, cannot be unlived, but if faced with courage, need not be lived again."
Maya Angelou

Chapter Three

AWAKENING

"The spirit, the will to win, and the will to excel are the things that endure. These qualities are so much more important than the events that occur."

Vince Lombardi

Self Discovery

"Naught is possessed, neither gold, nor land, nor love, nor life, nor peace, nor even sorrow nor death, nor yet salvation. Say of nothing: It is mine. Say only: It is with me."

D.H. Lawrence

*F*or comfort I began to cling to old friends back home in Fort Worth. Shane had been Tommy's best friend from the time they were old enough to walk—they were more like brothers than friends. He and his wife, Teresa, met when they were just thirteen. Teresa, Shane, and Tommy had been inseparable. Once I came into the picture, they lovingly welcomed me into their tight-knit family.

Shane would be the one to teach me how to play pool, put on a poker face, and deal with Tommy's unpredictable behavior. Teresa would lay by my side through sleepless nights and broken hearts. She was the first person I ran to when I found out I was pregnant with Kaden—and the one who was with me when I discovered Anistyn was on the way. Teresa met my plane right after Tommy's death. Shane remained by my side planning every step of the funeral. It was only natural for me to want to be close to my dear friends during this fragile time in my life.

I lived in Lubbock; they in Fort Worth. To ease the pain after the loss of Tommy, I spent most of my weekends driving three hundred miles to be with them. In the beginning, this was my only form of comfort. As time went on, I started to feel like an outsider. I saw that they could not comfort me any more than I was able to comfort them. It seemed as if I was a reminder of the past, and my presence brought with it the sting of Tommy's absence.

Truth be told, I was draining the life out of everyone around me. I was inconsolable. It was impossible for them, or anyone, to help me heal. I wanted to be a good friend, but trying to deal with my own grief made it difficult for me to be considerate of others. I was too lost to be a true companion.

My friends understood this. What they couldn't handle was the way I responded to anyone who did not meet my expectations. Something as simple as a wrong look could bring a cruel comment from me. My unpredictable behavior was much too difficult for even the best of friends to tolerate for any length of time.

I reached for joy anywhere I could find it. I got a makeover. I bought new clothes. I went out on a few dates. I had no idea what would make me happy, but I demanded that those around me fill the void. I wanted to be the center of attention. I wanted to be included. I expected everyone around me to be sensitive to my needs. In the end, I was left with disappointment and rejection. No person could live up to the high standards I held them to.

I had become so desperate to use my friends for comfort that I began to ignore the voice of my Spirit.

...Let them go.

…No, they are all I have.

...It's time to go your separate ways.

…No, I won't leave them behind.

...They can no longer help you.

I refused to accept that Tommy was the glue that held us together. I couldn't understand how I no longer seemed to fit into their lives.

For the most part, I was still trying to depend on outside relationships for love and acceptance. I sought comfort only from my friends as opposed to relying on God. Because I made companionship my first priority, I was unable to properly follow the positive help my Spirit was offering. I was coming to realize the impossibility of depending on two sources. If my dependency was on people, my Spirit would be unable to lift me up.

In spite of knowing this, I felt abandoned by my friends' inability to help me. I was alone, confused, and very angry. Most conversations ended in heated arguments. We were no longer able to support one another the way we had in the past. I was devastated. Out of anger, I came to the conclusion I could no longer hold our friendship together. I chose to let go of the one thing I wanted to grasp the most. Once I stopped instigating contact, the calls stopped completely. The door to my past closed, and I found my only companion to be that of my Spirit.

This was a very difficult time. I had been hurt by the very ones I believed would stand by my side and be there for me no matter what. Instead of looking at my circumstances through the eyes of my logic, I began to allow

God to show me a better way of interpreting the situation. *Their healing is separate from yours...forcing them to react to you the way you want is just as damaging as their asking you to perform to their standards...relationships will heal in time...first you must take care of you.*

As I began to accept the encouraging Voice inside of me, I realized how frequently my thoughts seemed to contradict one another. On one hand, I would want to scream; on the other, I knew I needed to calm down. At times I would want to stay home and sulk; simultaneously, I knew I needed to keep pressing ahead.

Why exactly was I receiving so many opposing viewpoints? Were my thoughts simply battling one another as a way of reasoning, or had I been getting ideas from more than one authority? How could I know for sure that I was receiving ideas from God as opposed to simply coming up with them on my own? I would soon discover much wisdom to be found in these seemingly innocent questions.

The Bible's simple statement, *every good and perfect gift comes from above* (James 1:17), gave me the answer I needed. The ideas encouraging me to take the higher road had indeed originated from my Spirit. I could choose to follow the assistance God was offering, or I could follow the perception of my logic. My happiness depended on which reasoning I chose to follow.

By separating my thoughts, I had begun teaching myself to recognize the voice of God's Spirit within me. My lack of happiness was never due to the fact that God failed to talk to me or offer assistance. I led an unfulfilled life because I wasn't listening. I began to recognize the potential of what God was offering. It was okay that I did not have all the answers; I would be led to them.

As I took this turn, I started to feel less discouraged and better suited to face each new day. I seized control of my healing by holding tight to my Source of love. I would feel uplifted and encouraged in every instance where I willingly gave over my negative thoughts and emotions to God. I would lie in bed and simply say, "God, I give my sorrow to You. I give my anger to You. I accept that I don't fully understand the circumstances surrounding my life. I give my disappointment to You. Please, God, help me continue to give everything to You."

The Face of Spirit

"We are not human beings on a spiritual journey. We are spiritual beings on a human journey."

Stephen R. Covey

Thinking positive thoughts was not only my connection to God, but my path to healing. My Spirit had been in the background subtly attempting to get me to choose a better way to live from the beginning. I could now see that I was destined to reach happiness because I had been given a Voice dedicated to leading me toward it.

I did not have to earn God's help by making my life a poster of perfection. I simply had to listen to the

Perfect Voice. If I could choose to follow my Spirit's help in all of my daily activities, the sky would be the limit on what I would be able to achieve.

It was not by chance that goodness found ways to interrupt my destructive thoughts. It was my Spirit offering assistance when I sensed an urge to stop and take calming breaths during heated arguments. It was my Spirit giving me strength to stand up for myself when I felt vulnerable. It was my Spirit urging me to rest during stressful moments. I learned to see my Spirit clearly by taking note of any and all thoughts that would lead me to a more peaceful resolution.

Now, I knew without a doubt that I had been placed on earth with a purpose. I did not yet know what that purpose was, but I certainly knew what it wasn't. It was not to sit around crying and wasting away living an unfulfilled life. Only by allowing Spirit and body to coexist as the single unit they were intended to be would I fully achieve happiness. *Not by might, nor by power, but by My Spirit says the Lord.* (Zechariah 4:6)

I was soon able to accept that Spirit can be denied but never extinguished. Nothing happens by chance. Every situation in my life had been allowed to take place for a reason. My pain and suffering had been molding me. My difficult circumstances were preparing me for the life I had been destined to live.

There had been a time when I believed that we had to follow a strict set of rules in order to follow God. Now I could see this was not so. By fully recognizing goodness comes from God, I was able to find Him in everyone, even those who had left me feeling alone and empty. For the first time, I began to look past the hurt others had caused me and see that God's love is available in many forms. If I could stop judging what I did not understand and start accepting people for who they were, I would be free.

As I sought to know my Spirit better and allow myself to be guided by this relationship, I began to see miraculous changes occur in my life. While in the midst of unimaginable pain, I began to experience peace beyond anything I could ever understand. My husband was dead and my closest friends were no longer a part of my life, yet I was happy.

I was also discovering new things about myself. In the past, I had taken up smoking as a way to calm my nerves. Now, I no longer felt the need to smoke. Before, I had thought that alcohol was necessary to have a good time. Now, I no longer felt the desire to drink. Relationships had been my way of finding comfort. Now, I was happiest being alone. Not all that long ago, I felt the need to surround myself with noise and projects. Now, I found myself searching for quiet moments of rest. I was definitely making progress.

Not surprisingly, the activities I had chosen to surround myself with were not the endeavors which would bring me the most joy. With little to no effort on my part, my Spirit began guiding me towards a lifestyle that more effectively suited my needs. I soon came to realize I was better off accepting the unconditional support from my Spirit than I had been by attempting to reach out and find comfort from other people.

Hearing from Spirit

"I think we all have a little voice inside us that will guide us. It may be God, I don't know. But I think that if we shut out all the noise and clutter from our lives and listen to that voice, it will tell us the right thing to do."

Christopher Reeve

*I*n the past, I had been warned that I would never find God if I wasn't willing to set aside time to pray and read the Bible. I had also been taught that I had to schedule appropriate "God time" each day. I had been anointed with oil, prayed for in the name of the Spirit, prophesied over by pastors, and openly rebuked in front of a church congregation. At times, I foolishly bought into the idea that, if I was able to live my life by the Book, I might one day be able to prove myself worthy enough to make it to heaven, find peace, and finally be with God.

Needless to say, I was never successful in finding a way to establish a meaningful relationship with God through rituals and ceremonies. They all left me feeling inferior.

On the other hand, I did feel as if God held me in high regard each moment I met with Him on an intimate level. That's why I made the decision to throw out the religious rules to seek an independent relationship with my Spirit. I intended to stop trying to mimic others and started to get very personal with God.

We all know that a healthy relationship can only be developed by listening and spending quality time with someone else. I couldn't expect to develop a relationship with my Spirit any differently. *Give attention to me, and keep quiet, and I will give you wisdom* (Job 33:33). Obviously, I could not expect to receive guidance if I wasn't willing to stop and listen to what God had to say. Simply saying a prayer was not the best way to nurture a relationship with my Helper. The most productive approach would be to live in a state of prayer—meaning, live in a state of awareness—so that I would be better able to pay attention.

I had to prioritize and create room for my Spirit to speak. And to do this, I first had to stop and listen. This was not an easy task. I had a full time job. I was a single parent providing for two small children. I was continually running Kaden from one activity to the next. I would arrive home with little time left to finish homework, feed kids, and have everyone bathed before bedtime. By the time I cleaned up the mess and crawled in for my own much needed rest, the baby would be awake yet again. I never stopped.

Little did I know, but my ability to find peace had been hindered by my seemingly innocent habit of listening to endless noise. If the television wasn't on, I would be listening to music. If the kids weren't screaming, I would be on the phone. I would stop what I was doing to pay attention to breaking news. I would turn off my phone and send the kids to bed so I could watch my favorite television show. I was constantly busy keeping up with my e-mail, blackberry, voicemail, and answering machine. I was placing effort in hearing from things that held minimal benefit. Little focus had been placed on activities that would help me achieve order. As a matter of fact, most of my actions created havoc.

There was so much going on around me that I could see how my Spirit would have difficulty getting me a message. All these distractions and interruptions had, in fact, become diversions that left no space for me to hear from my most important Communicator.

Once I became aware of this, I found that, by making the effort, I could find ample opportunities throughout the day to open up my mind. I began to complete as many tasks as possible in silence. I could make time for my Spirit to talk while I washed dishes, cleaned the house, cooked dinner, drove from place to place, or even as I waited to fall asleep.

I also discovered that the best time for me to focus on letting my Spirit communicate was in the early morning before the distractions cropped up. I would wake up early, go into another room, turn on soft classical music, and simply sit in peace. I would refrain from asking God for help. Instead, I would sit in stillness and wait. There were days when I would receive a message and others when I would not. But, I never left that space without a feeling of being nurtured and refreshed.

Going about my day in relative silence changed my life completely. I started to receive incredible insight once I made an appointment to hear God. Within a very short period of creating time to actively meditate, I began to have more wisdom and guidance to see solutions. I found myself making difficult decisions with certainty. I would stay peaceful when my children were anything but. I would complete tasks with more ease. Much to my surprise, life became less stressful, and joy began to replace sorrow.

I don't think it was simply my decision to cut out extraneous sound or wake up early that really made it possible for my Spirit to speak to me. I made a personal effort to listen. I chose to hear. My actions invited God's help. Regardless of the manner in which people of different religions or faiths go about hearing from God, I believe that if our intentions are good and our hearts are seeking ways to better hear from our Spirit, we will.

Spirit Versus Logic

"Peace is of God, you who are part of God are not at home except in His peace."

A Course in Miracles

*S*ometimes my thoughts were so numerous and random that I had a hard time telling whether they had come from my Spirit or my physical mind. The way I began to distinguish Spirit from logic was to stop and evaluate the tone.

I could see very clearly that Spirit's guidance would encourage me while my logic would have me react in fear. But there were other ways that helped me tell them apart as well.

My Spirit would answer with love, while my logic thrived on being critical. My Spirit reacted with excitement about future possibilities. My logic left me feeling afraid of uncertainty. My Spirit always encouraged me to give. My logic had me be selfish. My Spirit would help me forgive. My logic would convince me I had a right to seek out revenge. When I followed my Spirit, I always felt peaceful. Following my logic left me feeling anxious. My Spirit would have me react to others in a nurturing way, accepting differences and consoling those who were suffering. My logic had me believing it was only right to react judgmentally toward those who did not see as I did or who could cause me pain.

Another method I used to double-check whether my thoughts were spiritually motivated was to ask myself whether they brought about a sense of peace and encouragement. I made sure to only focus on solutions that empowered me, created feelings of joy, and would never result in harm.

In her book *Divine Guidance*, Doreen Virtue points out that physical thoughts often come across as whiny, nagging, irritating, and use "I" as the focus: *I can't do that…I don't have time for this…I don't feel well.* Doreen helped me see that the voice of Spiritual Guidance is quite different. This Voice is very direct and to the point. Spiritual messages never mix words and always aim to improved circumstances. The messages received from a Higher Self usually concentrate on "you": *You should relax…you should spend time with your children…you should donate to charity.*

As I received assistance from my Spirit, it was interesting to note how my logic would immediately try to hold me back. My Spirit might say…*you should keep quiet*, but my mind would argue…*I don't need to keep quiet…I know I am right.* If I followed the comfortable thoughts of my logic, I found myself lost in turmoil without fail. *You should attend that lecture …oh, I don't have time to attend any lec*ture*…you should go on a vacation…oh, I don't have the money to go on vacation.* It became obvious that nine times out of ten my logical thoughts argued with the voice of my Spirit and made excuses that would stop me from improving my life.

It wasn't long before I learned to wait for inner peace before making questionable decisions. Any and all choices lining up with my Spirit would be accompanied by peace. If I was unable to reach a point of knowing, I would hold off and spend time in prayer until peace accompanied my thoughts.

Unblocking Spiritual Communication

"Life has a bright side and a dark side, for the world of relativity is composed of light and shadows. If you permit your thoughts to dwell on evil, you yourself will become ugly. Look only for the good in everything so you absorb the quality of beauty."

Paramahansa Yogananda

I wanted the good life had to offer, yet much of the time I had chosen to focus on pain and negativity in order to reach it. This would never work. Happiness and joy would only be reached once I was able to focus on happiness and joy. I had placed so much of my focus on the pain and heartache I felt, my grief greatly multiplied.

I wanted to live an emotionally healthy lifestyle and realized I had to be willing to forgive the people I shut out of my life. Otherwise, I would be too bound up by my past to clearly see into my future. It would be impossible to hear from my Spirit if my perception was clouded with bitterness. *If we are not able to forgive, how do we expect to receive forgiveness ourselves? Forgive as quickly and completely as the Master forgave you, and regardless of what else you put on, wear love* (Colossian 3:13).

Choosing love, however, did not mean that I had to nurture every friendship that entered my life. I simply needed to learn how to let go of certain friends with love, essentially reaching a balance where I could release people along with any and all animosity.

I feared this vulnerability would open me up to pain, but that was not the case. As I started taking this step, I noticed that people began to take less advantage of me. My giving those around me the freedom to be themselves made it possible for everyone to be authentic. My friends no longer felt the need to walk on eggshells around me, and my relationships became entirely different. People were no longer forcing their actions to please me, and I enjoyed being able to witness my friends on a genuine level. I began to witness the amazing pureness that comes from allowing relationships to be organic.

By choosing to forgive not just Tommy but everyone in my life, I was able to accept relationships that were beneficial. I had been unable to recognize healthy friendships because I stubbornly held on to the wrong ones. Now that I was able to go with the flow, I was finding myself to be a much happier person.

Depression

"A lot of what passes for depression these days is nothing more than a body saying that it needs work."
Geoffrey Norman

*D*uring this time, it was obvious that I suffered many signs of depression. I had difficulty getting out of bed in the morning. I had become wickedly thin. My eyes remained permanently bloodshot. I withdrew from my surroundings. Doctors recommended that I begin a course of antidepressants.

I believe there are many instances of depression where medical intervention is a necessity. In fact, I have no doubt Tommy would be alive today if he had been willing to seek psychiatric care. But I wasn't sure whether this kind of treatment was best for me.

My suffering had been caused by circumstances and choices. Nothing about my behavior had been due to a chemical imbalance. I knew I had a right to take medication—it would help me feel better, if nothing else—but it would only provide a temporary fix.

I feared that masking my pain would give me only the appearance of joy. It seemed the best way to fully recover was to experience my sorrow. If I wanted to mature, I had to be willing to feel the pain.

At one time, I believed negativity offered zero benefits. Now I could see I had been wrong. The feelings I tried so hard to extinguish were, in fact, beneficial. My suffering had been warning me to slow down, pay better attention to my choices, and rely on my Spirit for help.

I needed to treasure my emotions and give them the freedom to finish their work by allowing them to run their course. It was time I learned to embrace my suffering. In other words, my pain was my medicine. I had to take it.

Understanding my mood was the key. I would experience Spirit's qualities of life—love, joy, peace, patience, kindness, goodness, faithfulness, gentleness, self-control—as long as I stayed tuned in to my Spirit. Encountering the opposite—pain, frustration, negativity—would be my warning to take notice.

I didn't need to fear my emotions. I only needed to learn how to properly read them. Pain had been a warning signal, not a sign of failure. Realizing this helped me change my lifestyle.

I made changes in the little things that had been affecting my day in a negative way. I stopped running myself into the ground by trying to make it appear I had everything under control. I began to enjoy time with my children instead of forcing myself to work around the house. I slept when I was tired. I recognized where I could find joy and gave myself the freedom to revel in each moment. I stopped forcing myself to do things that added to my depression and began to do more of what would lead me out of it.

Though I feared that making myself happy might bring disorder, that wasn't the case. Following my Spirit's advice to enjoy myself helped me become more accomplished. When my surroundings were peaceful, tasks were completed with ease. I found myself being able to complete projects that once seemed too burdensome.

In the midst of all that had been taking place around me, I began to realize how isolated I had become. A big part of my pain had been triggered by loneliness. I was discovering that depressed people like me have a difficult time letting others into their lives. Unfortunately, isolation only makes hard times more difficult.

I knew from past experience that God not only spoke to me individually, He enjoyed using others as well. God speaks through friendships. He offers a helping hand through relationships. I was missing much of God's assistance because I was afraid to allow new people into my life. Truth be told, I needed a friend. I needed to open myself up to new possibilities.

Then, an old companion appeared—Travis. He was one of Tommy's close childhood friends who always remained a mystery to me. He was very guarded and expected others to respect his boundaries, but in spite of his difficult nature, I knew I could depend on him if I needed anything, and because of that, I cared for him deeply. I could see from his relationship with Tommy that anyone fortunate enough to break through his protective shield would have the pleasure of knowing a very tender and genuine person indeed.

Travis seldom let anyone, most of all me, see an emotional side to him. I would be the last person to ever get his sympathy. I think this was the reason I could so easily trust him now. He was genuine. When it came to our friendship, he never pretended to be someone he was not.

Travis recently moved from California to New York to live near his daughter. Though he had a lot to deal with in his own life, he began calling to check on me every day. Of all people, he was the one hearing my desperation and doing his best to help me work through it. He had little money, but what he did have he offered to send. He used his vacation time to come to Texas and visit me and the kids. Travis became the one person I could freely confide in.

By allowing this new friendship, I had begun to do something constructive. It was not by chance that Travis came into my life at a very pivotal moment. I didn't necessarily depend on him to get me out of my depression, but I did value our friendship. I had no doubt God sent him to me for a reason.

Waiting on God

"God allows us to experience the low points of life in order to teach us lessons we could not learn in any other way. The way we learn those lessons is not to deny the feelings but to find the meanings underlying them."
Stanley Lindquist

*I*t was so important that I not allow myself to become discouraged if difficult circumstances didn't immediately improve. No matter my state of mind, some days didn't go as planned. I still lost my temper. I didn't always follow my Spirit's guidance right away. I seldom felt joy in uncomfortable situations. I easily became frustrated with myself and others. I continued feeling lost and confused.

It didn't seem to me that God was in the process of changing my life. But by remaining patient, giving God the details, and trusting in His perfect timing for the results to appear, I would eventually see everything fall into place. To help me keep from becoming frustrated when things didn't go my way, I began to compare my growth to that of nature.

When a tulip is planted, it doesn't immediately sprout. It takes time to settle into its new home, establish its roots, wait on the guidance of the sun, and gracefully emerge from the soil. Trying to rush the process would damage the plant, and the same went for me.

Most of my changes had begun to take place beneath the soil. I simply required a little more time for the changes to grow and bud. God had supernaturally set events into motion that I had yet to be made aware of. Despite appearances, my strength had begun to develop.

My mind could not comprehend the specific goodness of God's plan for me. Even though I had been willing to settle for a tumultuous life with my husband, God had not been so willing to allow me to accept this meager existence. I was not lost. I was simply in the midst of my transition. I was far from the disaster I appeared to be. God had been listening.

Living by the Spirit

"If you bring forth what is inside you, what you bring forth will save you. If you don't bring forth what is inside you, what you don't bring forth will destroy you."

Gospel of Thomas

*A*s I began to find comfort in following my Spirit's voice, I realized how aggressively I had begun to confront decisions in my life. I no longer took a passive approach to my daily activities. I was now able to recognize when my Spirit was talking, and I knew I was being encouraged to make changes. I began growing increasingly uncomfortable with my surroundings and felt a strong urgency for change. Because of this awareness, I had no doubt my world would soon be transformed. I could sense that there would be a move to a different place in my very near future.

I did wonder, however, if making a drastic change would be irresponsible of me. After all, I owned my own home, had a good job, and lived near a family that provided complete love and support. I was a single mother with two fragile children with zero savings.

Despite all the obvious reasons to stay, I yearned to follow my Spirit and experience the life I knew awaited me. I realized this desire for change was my Spirit pushing me to make a life-altering choice. I was frightened by this overwhelming discovery, but I knew the time had come for me to start living through the direction of my Spirit. I would never achieve all that life had to offer if I was unable to take chances. I believed my Spirit could be trusted and made up my mind not to let fear hold me back.

By honestly examining my desires, I realized a dream I'd never thought possible. My entire world revolved around life in the South. I had never ventured too far from home and had remained dependant on the same circle of friends. I could no longer find comfort here. I wanted to experience diversity. I wanted to expose my children to a different way of living. I wanted change. I dreamed of living in a place where I could discover myself and be free to do things my own way. *You should move to New York.*

There is no way God would allow me this luxury… no dream this big could ever become my reality. My mind would move back and forth from the foolishness of my desire to start fresh and the reality of my situation. My Spirit was pushing me to make a move toward fulfilling my dreams. My logic faithfully tried to hold me back.

To clear my head, I began to spend time examining myself to confirm I was on the right path. I had to know for sure where this desire to pack up my children and leave our familiar and safe home had come from. Was I running away from my pain? Was I being selfish? The answer to my questions was clearly no. I knew deep down that my Spirit had begun directing me to a new reality. My desires rose from a place of purely trusting in my Spirit's wisdom to show me how to attain the prosperity I had been praying for. By turning my desires over to the more important things given by the Spirit, I would be pointed to an even better way of life. (1 Corinthians 12:31)

My logical thoughts did not make it easy for me to believe such a huge change could be a good thing. I had been very close to living paycheck to paycheck, so the financial means and security to support the move weren't available. Aside from Travis living up North, I would be completely on my own. I didn't know how I would get my kids off to school while working a full-time job. I worried that my limited education would hold me back. I didn't see how I could afford a house and hadn't the slightest clue where I would live.

None of my reasoning came up with a way to make this move a reality. Luckily, my Spirit quickly interrupted my negativity: *Of course it's impossible...most big steps are impossible when you try to figure them out on your own...let go, I have the power to do anything...if you trust in Me, there is nothing we can't accomplish.*

Through much consideration, I settled on the fact that God had everything under control. I didn't have to struggle with worrying about finances, jobs, my children, or anything else. There were two choices available to me. I could trust in myself and the familiarity of my life that had been put in place, or I could rest in the truth that God didn't need my current securities. If I honestly trusted in God and in His provisions for me, I had to let go of my safety net and grab onto Him. Money and circumstances could no longer dictate my life. If I was serious about discovering how good my world could be, I had to jump in and trust my Spirit.

I would travel to New York during the next few months to familiarize myself with the area. Once I compared the cost of living from Lubbock to New York City, I could clearly see the impossibility of my situation. I would be selling a house for a little more than a hundred thousand dollars and moving to a place where a bathroom renovation could cost that much. One could barely go out to dinner for less than fifty dollars a meal.

I also discovered that, as much as I loved New York, it was too hectic of an environment in which to raise my children comfortably. There would be no running outside to ride bikes or play in the yard; daycare facilities were full; and schools were very different from the ones Kaden had been accustomed to.

Regardless of how absurd everything seemed, each time I tried to drop the dream of moving away, my Spirit would pick it back up and remind me not to let physical roadblocks discourage me. **I was to look at these roadblocks for what they were: put in place to help me see the power of God in action, to confirm what I was capable of if I surrendered and let my Spirit point the way.**

If God can do all things, I can do all things while allowing His power to work through me. Moving my family across the country was a tiny thing to achieve in God's eyes. If He created me, He could easily care for me. After all, *if my Father in heaven gives the birds food to eat, how much more would he care for me?* (Matthew 6:26). It was time for me to completely let go and allow my Spirit to direct my life.

"The most important thing to remember is this: To be ready at any moment to give up what you are for what you might become."

W.E.B. Du Bois

Chapter Four

SURRENDER

*"When you have compassion and surrender
to your own heart, you are surrendering to
the hidden power in your heart, God. You
are surrendering to love, because God is
Love, the cohesive force of the universe that
connects us all. Surrender is not just a religious concept; it's a power tool for listening
to the voice of your spirit and following its
directions. When you surrender your head
to your heart, you allow your heart to give
you a wider, higher, intelligence perspective.
Remember the phrase, 'The real teacher is
within you.' Very simply, that teacher is to be*

found in the common sense of

your own heart."

Sara Paddison,
The Hidden Power of the Heart

Letting Go

"The possibility of stepping into a higher plane is quite real for everyone. It requires no force of effort or sacrifice. It involves little more than changing our ideas about what is normal."

Dr. Deepak Chopra

he outcome of my future depended on my willingness to make some very difficult choices. One road ignited passion, the other convenience. I was beginning to heal and settle into a safe pattern in Texas. My life was simple, pleasant, and I had the opportunity to raise my children in a stable, loving environment.

Moving to New York definitely would be risky. Living there would be full of uncertainty, and I would have to reestablish myself completely. But I felt I would have no regrets. If things didn't go as planned, I could always move back to Texas. If they did go smoothly, I would be living life on my own terms. I would have the opportunity to learn new things about myself. I would be free.

Still, I was afraid to let go, fearful that I might not be able to accomplish my dreams. This was my thinking, even though my past had proven the opposite to be true. The times I had been able to let go, miracles happened. When I stopped struggling to be the wife I thought would please my husband, I became someone he enjoyed being around. As I let go of trying to heal my son's heartache, I watched him blossom back into a healthy child. Once I quit fearing the loss of friendships, quality relationships formed around me.

The part of letting go that involved accepting my Spirit's guidance and relinquishing control to Him had created the most progress in the past. Once I was willing to let Him reveal a new reality, God showed me what I was capable of achieving. I had to stop struggling to make my life fit inside a preconceived mold. I had to surrender my wasted effort so I would be able to gain new perspective.

And more: I had to let myself make the changes my heart was telling me were necessary even though my head didn't understand. I had to be willing to move forward even though my surroundings might not appear safe. I had to accept that I would not know how the story would end. I had to let go of fear and allow faith to carry me into the dark.

Letting go did not mean that I would no longer struggle. It did not mean I would never again experience pain. Letting go simply gave God the authority to make decisions on my behalf. Pain and sorrow might still remain, but these were simply side effects of growth and change.

Hope

"Consult not your fears, but your hopes and your dreams. Think not about your frustrations, but about your unfulfilled potential. Concern yourself not with what you tried and failed in, but with what it is still possible for you to do."

Pope John XXIII

I had known hopelessness all too well, but now I had to have hope and to believe in victory. Without hope, I would never live a prosperous life. With it, nothing could stop me.

I began letting myself look to the future. I could see myself moving to New York. I could see myself making a good living. I could see myself residing in a comfortable home. I could see myself having fun and making new friends. I could see myself happy.

This hope was not merely wishful thinking. It was a vision my Spirit had given to help bring me back to life. Hope was God's encouragement. In other words, the hopefulness that had begun to spark my excitement was God's way of speaking to me.

God would not give me a dream if He were not willing to help me reach it. He would not move me to New York to simply have me become helpless. The problem had not been God's faithfulness. My fearing change, loneliness, and lack of money had kept me from trusting. I had been too afraid of failure to take hold of my dreams. If I sincerely wanted to reach new heights, I had to trust that obstacles could not keep anything out of my grasp. God would get me through as long as I remained faithful, followed His guidance, and trusted Him completely.

Let us hold firmly to the hope we claim to have. The one who promised is faithful (Hebrews. 10:23). Hope was my heavenly reward revealed.

Fear

"Fear does not have any special power unless you empower it by submitting to it."

Les Brown

In order for me to hang on to hope, I had to first let go of my fear. Fear was something I had built my life on. My home was bought because I feared living too far away from my family. I worked at my job because I feared I was unqualified to find better. I married because I feared life without Tommy would be too painful. I had children because I feared being alone. I followed advice because I feared what people would think of me if I didn't listen. I let my family ideals be my own because I feared their disapproval. I compared myself to those around me because I feared my life would never measure up to theirs.

Fear would only keep me consumed with the same problems I had encountered in the past. The fear of not knowing what I would end up with in New York or elsewhere threatened to hold me back. It terrified me to think how vulnerable I would be once I left Texas. What if I couldn't make enough money? What if I didn't succeed? What if I ruined my children's lives as well as my own?

I simply had no choice but to find the strength to ignore this reasoning and begin to make decisions that were based on conviction. I had to lighten up and learn to be flexible. I could no longer let fear hold me hostage. If I wanted change, I had to want it enough to trust that God would get me there.

Even though I felt anxious and had conflicting thoughts, I had to find the resolve to move forward. Joy was on the other side of my grief. Abundance was on the other side of my scarcity. Friendship was around the corner from my loneliness. Great faith was around the corner from my concern. All that I desired to be was simply around the corner from where I was today.

My best option was to surrender all that was unstable and let it fall away. I could no longer depend on my friends, my family, my job, or my home to fill the void inside of me. Control and safety were illusions. My only guarantee was God's protection.

When I thought of moving and leaving my old life behind, I began to feel much lighter. Joy and excitement took over me as I sensed an inner push to go ahead and make the change. When I considered staying, I felt confined and less alive. In spite of the sense of security that my job, family, and home brought, my life was unfulfilling. My heart knew it was time to move on.

Darkness

"When you get to the end of all the light you know and it's time to step into the darkness of the unknown, faith knows that one of two things shall happen: either you will be given something solid to stand on, or you will be taught how to fly."

Edward Teller

*O*wning a home had been a dream I had worked hard to achieve. But if I moved to New York, I would have to pay more than $1 million to buy something similar. Once I left Texas, I simply wouldn't be able to maintain the standard of living I had become accustomed to. I took pride in being a homeowner. I also was proud that I had been able to invest my money wisely. The thought of letting go of these accomplishments pained me.

To add insult to injury, I had no equity in my house. I would be lucky to break even after paying realtors, taxes, and fees. And it would cost so much more to rent in New York that I doubted I would ever be able to save enough for another down payment.

Instead of fearing my uncertain future, I would wait for my Spirit to help open the doors that would make it possible for me to own again once the time was right. I had to find the bravery to approach life head on and press forward in spite of my lacking the resources to do it in the way I wanted.

I didn't need to see to the end of the road because my Light had taken my hand and was safely leading me forward. Owning a home did not define me. I finally let my disappointment take a backseat and made peace with the fact that my Intuition was a more trustworthy source of guidance.

There were no guarantees that following my Spirit would get me everything I wanted. The only assurance I had was that there were stronger hands holding me than I could ever understand. My life would be full and complete in spite of my reaching a destination that would be unlike what I had envisioned in the beginning.

That is why it was so important for me to let go. I had to stop fighting for the wrong things in order to achieve the right ones. Material gain was nothing compared to finding peace, achieving happiness, and living fulfilled.

It took great strength for me to allow myself the freedom to feel uncertainty. Now I could see that confronting my fear was the only way to recreate my life.

Being Lead by Spirit

"Turn toward the light, for the little spark in you is part of a light so great that it can sweep you out of all darkness forever."

A Course in Miracles

I had already come to the conclusion that New York City was not the place I wanted to raise my children. I went back to look at other places nearby, venturing to Connecticut, where I instantly fell in love with the state.

During my first visit, I witnessed one of the most beautiful summers I had ever seen. The weather was perfect. Trees surrounded every house and lined every street. On one side of Norwalk, there were lakes so amazingly peaceful that they appeared to have come straight out of a storybook. On the other side were oceans and beaches that offered the kids a great place to play.

I absolutely loved the area. I would have plenty to do, and, unlike in Manhattan, I would be able to park my car for free. Here, I would be within driving distance of New York and still be able to enjoy the comforts of the country. Though I didn't know the area, I knew from the moment I arrived that this would be my home.

I decided to follow my Intuition and confess my plans of moving to my very disappointed and worried family. My choice to follow my Spirit, pick up my children, and relocate to the other side of the country made everyone think I had truly gone mad. I knew nothing about the area, but I knew without a doubt that God was calling me to this place for a reason. The physical hurdles didn't matter. I prayed, waited, and stayed hopeful, knowing that if my desires were flowing out of my unity with my Spirit, the obstacles would diminish and the move would be made possible.

A business associate knew a few people in Connecticut and brought a potential employment situation to my attention at a lighting showroom that was joined to an electrical supply house. Due to a recent corporate takeover, the lighting side of the company had begun to fall apart, while the electrical supply side was thriving.

The new owners considered restructuring the lighting department but were having trouble finding the right person to manage the transition. My experience in lighting, home decorating, and business management placed me as the number-one candidate.

I quickly flew to New York for an interview but was unable to land the job. The main reservation in hiring me was the fact that I still lived in Texas. Unfortunately, the company was not prepared to help me relocate. The only way they would change their mind and consider me for the position was if I established a permanent residence in the area.

Before leaving the interview, I was warned not to base my decision to move on the availability of this job. The future of the company still remained in question. That made my trust in my Intuition even more difficult for me to put my faith in. I would have to take a huge gamble, one that would not be easy considering that the welfare of my children would be at stake. If this job worked out, it would pay enough to support us. If it fell through, it would put me in a bind.

I had other possible leads. One way or another, I would find work. The problem was the pay. No other job offered me what I needed to live comfortably in the New England economy.

House hunting brought other obstacles. Homes in Connecticut were so expensive that I would be lucky to break even once I sold my home in Texas. Looking at rental property brought just as much uncertainty.

The idea of paying more than two thousand dollars a month for a small non-air-conditioned home made me cringe.

Every decision I made could be compared to closing my eyes, jumping into a black pit, and relying on a miracle to grant a safe landing. When fear began to take hold, I would remind myself that God's eyes were on my path; nets had been secretly placed in the way in which I would go (Psalm 142:3).

The reality of my situation was daunting. My education was limited and the job market was very competitive. Fairfield County just happened to be one of the most expensive in the nation and the cost of living was beyond my grasp.

On another note, my relationship with Travis had become complicated. Our friendship was becoming something more intimate and neither of us was clear on how to deal with these new feelings. We were both hesitant and a bit uncomfortable at times. However, we were learning how to let go of our concerns and let God handle the details. I was actually glad to have the opportunity to look ahead towards the possibility of starting a new relationship. Travis and I were both eager to see where our feelings might lead us.

Aside from Travis, I would be my own companion. It would be me and the kids, no sitters, no social calendar, and none of my old friendships to provide comfort. If I was unable to welcome the companion inside of me, I was going to be a very lonely individual.

I began to think that God had a real sense of humor when it came to my life. Observing the way He worked was frustrating, to say the least. I knew in my heart that all my needs would be met, but I had no idea how.

Nevertheless, a year and a half after Tommy's death, I sold my home, making a fifty dollar profit. I faithfully believed the job I had been hoping for would come through as I committed to renting a decent house in a quiet Norwalk neighborhood. I left the kids in Texas to spend one last summer with their grandparents, while I moved two thousand miles away from anything remotely familiar. All the while I prayed that God's safety nets would hold strong.

Travis came down to help me move, and together we drove a U-Haul to Connecticut. The two-day trip actually took three. By the time we reached our destination, both of us were absolutely exhausted. Unfortunately, there would be no resting because the furniture would have to be unloaded before we had a place to sit. Looking around, I could plainly see that I had my work cut out for me.

My little three-bedroom house looked like a red barn and was very quaint. But it sat in the middle of a large yard full of trees, stumps, and rocks. I would need someone to help me maintain the property. The trees were beautiful, but once fall arrived, the leaves would fall from morning until night. And during snow season, I would need help shoveling and plowing, or my walks would be covered in ice, and my car would get stuck in the driveway.

I had been well aware that I had less than four thousand dollars to my name and a monthly rent payment of twenty-two hundred dollars due in three weeks. But, there were other financial obligations—like the cost of heating my home with fuel—that I had been unprepared for. I had never even seen a fuel tank before! Add to that the cost of day care, groceries, and gas, which were nearly double what I had been used to paying.

Life

"Without darkness nothing comes to birth, as without light, nothing flowers."

May Sarton

*W*hat had happened, I realized, was that God withheld information as a way of protecting me as opposed to hindering me. If I had too much insight into the future, I might allow my faulty logic to take over. I would force things to happen instead of waiting for them to unfold. God knew the danger in this, and kept most of the details concealed from me.

It was actually good that I didn't always know what I had been walking into. If I had known the cost, there is a big possibility I would have backed away all too soon.

Moving across the country with hardly any money was extreme, to say the least. That was my journey, and it most certainly is not for everyone. We aren't expected to move mountains in one day. We grow by starting small. Few people will need to go through the extreme of losing a husband and having to uproot their life in order to spiritually emerge.

For the most part, we simply need to make minor adjustments in our daily activities to improve a negative lifestyle. If we are in the midst of a conversation and feel led by Spirit to say something that logic doesn't agree with, try surrendering logic and saying it anyway. If we feel led by Spirit to give money to the homeless but hear our logical voice reminding us that we don't have enough money to give, give in faith anyway. If our Spirit is nudging us to apologize after an argument where we were are clearly not at fault, let go of pride and allow Spirit to lead us to apologize.

In taking these small steps of faith, we will begin to see benefits and, in time, will become more comfortable in taking leaps. With practice, this will become natural. We will welcome the opportunity to take a chance on life. We will revel in opening a new business or starting an unconventional love affair. We will live with abandonment and, in turn, experience more than we ever dreamed possible.

Our Spirit knows what will make us happy because our Spirit knows our purpose in life. We find true and lasting happiness once we stop struggling to create it. It is interesting to note that we really don't know what will bring us happiness. We think we do. We believe that if others would treat us better, then we would be happy. If we got that promotion, then we would be happy. If we had more time for ourselves, then we would be happy. If we got married, then we would be happy. If we had a child, then we would be happy. When our goals are achieved, we find the happiness and satisfaction gained are short-lived. We always want more.

When we drop our defenses, the power of the Universe is able to take charge. Nothing can stand in our way of accomplishing our goals when this magnificent force is holding the reins. We will feel the weight of life's burdens lift from our shoulders as soon as we stop pushing against the current. We will find relationships working themselves out with ease by our willingness to walk away from conflict. Once we become willing to let go, there are no limits to what our Spirit is able to accomplish.

Today's lot in life will not determine where we will end up tomorrow. Circumstances will always work out one way or another. Life moves on, and good or bad, situations are forever changing. If we allow God to navigate our lives, we will discover obstacles no longer working against us, but refining us. We will experience peace through adversity as we rely on a loving Father to wrap us in His arms and carry us through.

"Whatever you do, you need courage. Whatever course you decide upon, there is always someone to tell you that you are wrong. There are always difficulties arising that tempt you to believe your critics are right. To map out a course of action and follow it to an end requires some of the same courage that a soldier needs. Peace has its victories, but it takes brave men and women to win them."

Ralph Waldo Emerson

Chapter Five

FAITH

"Man often becomes what he believes himself to be. If I keep on saying to myself that I cannot do a certain thing, it is possible that I may end by really becoming incapable of doing it. On the contrary, If I have belief that I can do it, I shall surely acquire the capacity to do it even if I may not have it at the beginning."

Mahatma Gandhi

Uncertainty

*"Our doubts are traitors and make us lose the good
we oft might win, by fearing to attempt."*
William Shakespeare

I had done what most people would consider un-
thinkable. I had chosen to live on faith, which made
backing out very difficult. I allowed myself to become
helpless, trusting that my helplessness would actually
turn my life around. To most, this would be considered
lunacy. To me, it was perfectly sane.

In spite of my drive and determination, the facts
surrounding my circumstances weighed heavily on my
thoughts. Truth be told, no amount of faith changed the
fact that I had yet to secure a job. Each passing day
proved my future would be anything but promising. It
was becoming increasingly difficult for me to accept
that God was capable of doing a better job of taking
care of me than I could do on my own.

In my mind, unemployment equaled insecurity. Not
knowing for certain how I would pay the bills and feed
my children was worrisome to say the least. To worry
was natural. To trust was impossible. Unfortunately,
fretting would never help improve my circumstances. I
had to somehow find a way to maintain a positive

outlook, keep trusting God, and patiently wait on His timing.

To accomplish this, I began making every effort to focus on anything but what was lacking in my life. Instead of fretting about what was missing, I worked at being productive. I focused on the task that lay directly in front of me.

I used my free time to unpack and organize the house. I drove around the city to familiarize myself with my new surroundings. I visited schools and chose a day care facility to assure a stable routine for my children. I forced myself to go along as if everything was as it should be. I gave myself less time to worry about the future by doing all that I could for the moment.

The plan was to wait a few weeks before going back to pick up the kids in Texas, but money was running low. Since I had yet to find work in Connecticut, I decided to pick them up earlier than planned. This way, I could go back to Texas and earn extra income by working for my family. I knew I had to remain flexible if I was going to be led to a solution. I sent out a few resumes before leaving and anxiously waited for the right door to open in my absence.

Having the extra work helped ease my hungry bank account, but this comfort was short-lived. Three months of waiting passed, and the owners of the lighting showroom had yet to answer my calls. I brought the kids back to Connecticut realizing that the career I had counted on was never going to work out.

I was trying to find another source of income, but even though I had a few job interviews, nothing close to promising developed. I would tell myself I needed to take advantage of any offer that came along, but I felt something pull me back each time I considered settling on a less than ideal solution. **I knew from past experience that this pull was, in fact, my Spirit's way of helping me determine the right path.** So, I waited to make a final decision.

Not knowing how I was going to provide for my family left me in a state of panic. How cruel of God to have so little interest in helping me find employment. The fact that He left me vulnerable after my faith in Him moved me across the country angered me to no end. Because things hadn't turned out the way I envisioned, my courage was quickly wearing thin.

What is Faith?

"What we see depends mainly on what we look for."
                                        John Lubbock

*T*wo scriptures stood out as I began to take a deeper look into my fear and worry. The first was Romans 12:3, *God hath dealt to every man the measure of faith.* Here I could see that faith was indeed a gift from God. There was nothing I could do to produce it on my own.

The second was Romans 10:17, *Faith cometh by hearing, and hearing by the word of God.* Still, I was having a hard time trusting that everything would be okay.

I could clearly see that faith had been given to all and was received by hearing, but I wasn't clear exactly

how this knowledge could help improve my circumstances. Then it hit me. How do people hear the word of
God? Reading the Bible and other spiritual texts is one
way to hear. Going to church and listening to a sermon
is yet another. However, truly hearing occurs on a deeper level. To actually hear the voice of God, one must
pay close attention to the Voice of their Spirit. In the
end, it all comes back to being willing to surrender.

To hold tight to faith, I had to rest in the fact that I
had found truth by following the Voice that dwelt inside
of me. Preachers, writers, parents, friends, or any other
outside influence could never be my supreme authority
for choosing a course of action. I could no longer judge
truth by the state of my circumstances or the persuasion
of others. Instead, I had to trust that the Voice speaking
within my soul held the answers, period.

I had to keep my eyes focused on my Spiritual goals
regardless of what problems surrounded me. I could not
be motivated to change course simply because things
were not going as planned. I would misjudge any situation if I tried to find the truth by what my eyes were
limited to seeing. My Spirit was able to see the big picture; my logic, only bits and pieces.

The lack of a job did not foreshadow failure. In fact,
despite unbelievable odds, there was never a necessity in
my home that went unmet. Food was always on the table.
The kids were clothed. We had a warm roof over our heads.
Every need I had in the moment had been provided for. I
didn't have a job, but I was taken care of nonetheless.

In instances where I chose to believe I was safe, I
would find myself resting safely. Take the time I put

my house on the market. I knew the selling price was too high, and I was running the risk of not being able to sell before I intended to move. I trusted my Intuition and miraculously found a buyer at just the right moment. This happened yet again when I qualified to rent my new home in Connecticut—which should have been impossible considering that I had yet to secure a job and had barely enough cash to cover the deposit.

In either of the above instances, if I had tried to force things to happen, the outcome would have been less favorable. If I gave into my fear, I would have lost too much money at the closing. Or I would have found myself settling in Connecticut on a less expensive home and living in an unsafe part of town.

By letting past lessons be my guide, I could now see that no amount of force would change my current situation. The more I fought and tried to take back the reigns, the harder I battled with my circumstances. Acceptance created flow and ease. Applying pressure only created more stress.

Every person operates by faith. Every person's life is created by their use of faith. Faith had always been at work in my life. The question hadn't been whether or not I had faith. It had been how I chose to apply that faith. Once I grasped this truth, I was able to see how I had continually misused my faith to achieve the exact opposite of what I desired.

I had begun placing too much effort in believing the negative to be true as opposed to believing the positive could be true as well. It would be my downfall once again if I continued to affirm that I would be unable to find a job or that my needs would go unmet. To succeed, I had no other choice but to conclude that, despite appearances, God had everything under control.

Faith, very simply stated, was the truth in which I chose to believe. I could believe in harm, or I could believe in protection. I could believe in scarcity, or I could believe in abundance. I could believe in sickness, or I could believe in health. **The direction of my faith would set the foundation for the reality I would experience.** I could take hold of my God-given power to inherit the life I was meant to live by shifting my belief to His promise of reaching my dreams. In other words, **I would live my beliefs.**

Approaching life the same way each day would continue to produce the same results. The person who continually talks about sickness is always sick. The one who wallows in self-pity over relationships that never improve is the one who continually experiences difficult relationships. Those who constantly complain about lack of money are the ones who never seem to have enough money. *If you believe, you will receive* (Matthew 21:22). Once again, my faith would produce what I believed.

"If you change the way you look at things, the things you look at change" (Dr. Wayne Dyer). Despite counter evidence, I had to continue to believe I would be taken care of. *Blessed are they that have not seen, and yet have believed* (Hebrews 11:1). When I was capable of believing in what I could not see, I would then be able to create a new reality.

Disappointment

*"All prayers are answered if we are willing to admit
that sometimes the answer is "no."*

Anonymous

*M*y requests had yet to be granted; I found myself discouraged. The truth was clear. Despite what I
believed, the possibility of never receiving some of my
demands would forever remain present. In order to
overcome my disappointment, I first had to acknowledge that the world was more of a spiritual place than a
physical one. In other words, to find true success I had
to grasp that life was larger than temporary gain.

It was not adequate that wealth and material achieve-
ment had become foremost on my list of desires. But this
did not mean abundance would be withheld because I
was undeserving. As prized children of God we are all
meant to receive the best that life has to offer. However,
the best of life may mean living without material wealth
in order to achieve something greater. As I've said before, God knows best what will bring us happiness.
Sometimes we have petitioned the wrong request. To
find ultimate happiness, I had to first come into align-
ment with my Spirit's aspirations.

Though I was very disappointed that I hadn't found a
job, I now believe that God did not want me to go to work
immediately. For starters, the children needed a calm environment for the move to be a positive change. If I had followed my logic and taken the first available position, I

would have been unable to spend time helping them adjust to the move. If I had taken matters into my own hands, I would have forced the children into the hands of strangers while I frantically worked at a low-paying job trying to make ends meet. And I would have eventually needed to take a second job just to pay the bills.

God had not merely been interested in meeting my deepest needs, but in meeting the needs of my children as well. When we let God take control, everyone profits. I truly believe that it was because of God's love for me that I was still unemployed.

I was learning to accept that certain requests would only be withheld for my own benefit. The key to peace was finding contentment where I stood and believing that at this very moment, I was experiencing exactly what God felt would bring me the best possible results—even if that meant being jobless for now.

The Power of Thought

"What you think, you become."

Buddha

I could see my circumstances in a different light once I began to believe all of my needs were truly on the way. Each time a negative thought entered my mind, I would immediately attempt to counter it: *This is never going to work...yes it is, the timing just isn't right. I have no money in the bank...I'm not out on the streets. There is no way I* can afford groceries this week...the kids love peanut butter and jelly sandwiches for dinner.

I did everything I could to help redirect my thoughts in a more positive direction. I began to focus my attention on the outcome instead of the current state of deficiency. I took my focus away from what I did not want and directed it toward what I did want. Anytime I became discouraged, I made a list of all that I had to be grateful for and focused on my blessings. Doing this helped me realize that, since the basic needs of my children and I had never gone unmet, I had been cared for unconditionally.

All of my anxiety began to disappear once I began to place my attention on my blessings as opposed to setbacks. **What I could see in the natural eye was not the finished product. Just because I didn't know the way out of my problems did not mean a way out did not exist.**

The Power of Words

"It is a well-known fact that one comes, finally, to believe whatever one repeats to oneself, whether the statement be true or false. If a man repeats a lie over and over, he will eventually accept the lie as truth. Moreover, he will believe it to be the truth. Every man is what he is because of the dominating thoughts which he permits to occupy his mind."

Napoleon Hill

*W*ords in themselves would never create the positive results I had been looking for. They would, however, help calm my anxiety and take my thoughts to higher levels. I soon realized that speech was an effective tool for promoting change. As I began to speak about circumstances in a positive way, my thoughts began to align effectively.

I began to repeat positive statements about my future: *God did not bring me this far to let me down now...I am safe in spite of what I may feel...changing my way of thinking is going to change my life.* I made a point of avoiding such words as "can't," "never," or "impossible." Instead, I spoke in expectation of my dreams and desires. This was a revolutionary step in creating positive life changes.

As I took a closer look at the words I used, I could see that my life had literally produced more of what I heard myself repeating and less of what I wanted. If I complained about my children acting up, my kids seemed to follow my rules less and less. If I repeated that I was too tired to complete a project, I remained weary and lethargic. I had not been helping myself find a job because I had never ceased complaining about the lack of one. I was finding proof that negative statements, in any form, were extremely damaging when spoken on a regular basis.

On the flip side, I had been able to successfully move because I had never spoken doubtfully about the possibility. My children were happy and healing quickly from our tumultuous past because I wouldn't allow myself to speak of any other outcome. I truly found encouragement by monitoring the language I used.

My words did, in fact, direct my thoughts. The words I chose to speak were key factors in determining the kind of life I would live. **If I didn't want it, I stopped speaking about it**. *A fool's mouth is his ruin, and his lips are a snare to his soul* (Proverbs 18:7).

The Power of Emotions

"The feeling is often the deeper truth, the opinion the more superficial one."

Augustus William Hare

I was, in a sense, looking for ways in which to manipulate my emotions to enable them to rise from a state of hopelessness to a place of encouragement. Negativity was the destructive misdirection of faith, while hope was a sign of productive faith. I found emotions to be a great gauge to help ensure that I believed in what I wanted as opposed to what I didn't have.

If I began complaining, my emotions made me feel hopeless, depressed, angry, or bitter. These unfavorable feelings were my wake-up call. They were sounding off to let me know that I had been sending my faith in the wrong direction.

The way for me to get out of any depression was to listen to it. I had to learn how to hear what it had to say. My emotions were telling me that my actions were not serving me well. I had to uncover the cause of my negative emotions and begin to take the steps that would lead me in another direction.

Among the positive steps I took: Instead of being miserable about my lack of work, I began to send out resumes. If I was feeling overwhelmed, I would let myself take a day off from hunting. To offset some of my loneliness, I got a cat. I collected pennies in a jar instead of complaining about the lack of money. I made it a priority to take care and nurture my emotional state. These simple actions of trying to improve my circumstances gave my faith a boost.

And they helped my positive emotions to grow. Hope fed hope. Joy fed joy. Love fed love. As I focused on solutions rather than problems, I was able to watch my life thrive with excitement and blessings.

The Power of Prayer

"You can tell the size of your God by looking at the size of your worry list; the longer your list, the smaller your God."

Author Unknown

Continually praying over and over again asking God for the same thing was more proof I did not believe He had answered me. There is nothing wrong with seeking God. As I began to open my eyes, I could see that a new approach to my seemingly unanswered prayers might be in order.

With a close relationship comes complete trust. If I believed God heard my prayers, I should no longer feel the need to keep asking. Once I asked, I should be able to place the requests at His feet and know that He would acknowledge my needs. Instead of repeating my prayers over and over again, I began to instead give thanks.

Rather than beg God for money and work, I would thank Him for the right job that would come any day now. I thanked Him for the bills that were paid and the food that was on the table. I thanked Him for His perfect timing. I thanked Him for helping me wait patiently. I thanked Him for His commitment to me. I thanked Him for never leaving or forsaking me. I thanked Him for listening to my prayers and caring for my broken heart.

I deliberately chose to be thankful for the favors I had been given instead of allowing myself to be angry over what appeared to be lacking. **By giving thanks, I created forward motion.** Asking was step one. Believing was step two. Being thankful was step three. Seeing the result would be step four. The uncertainty of tomorrow still existed, but each new day would reveal answers of its own.

Childlike Faith

"Know you what it is to be a child? It is to be something very different from the man of today. It is to have a spirit yet streaming from the waters of baptism; it is to believe in love, to believe in loveliness, to believe

in belief; it is to be so little that the elves can reach to whisper in your ear; it is to turn pumpkins into coaches, and mice into horses, lowness into loftiness, and nothing into everything, for each child has its fairy godmother in its own soul."

Francis Thompson

*T*o make it through the day with fewer bumps and bruises, children need to follow instructions and trust that the wisdom granted to them by authority, primarily their parents, is worth listening to. They may not realize it, but they live by Spirit and rely entirely on faith for survival. They believe in the good that life has to offer. They are free to fail and do not stop simply because of a few obstacles. They do not fear trouble but look to new experiences as exciting adventures. As long as they remain in a safe environment, they expect to be lovingly cared for and do not expect disaster. What an amazing existence! When we adults choose to submit to Spirit, we, too, are in a safe environment and can expect the same.

We come into life with the heart of a child. We are dependent and happy. Unfortunately, somewhere down the line, we abandon dependency. Pain causes us to believe our body to be weak. Disappointment motivates us to doubt victory. People have let us down so we feel alone. We came into life with an unconscious connection to the spiritual goodness around us, but have failed to recognize it for whatever reason.

I was finding out that it was possible to once again live with the peace that trusting in the childlike bond with the Spirit creates. My Spirit had the power to free me from doubt so I could trust that each new day would bring goodness and blessings. *Unless you accept God's kingdom in the simplicity of a child, you will never get in* (Mark 10:15).

My Spirit had been calling me to get back to this innocence, to love without expecting something in return, to embrace every day as if it were my last, to lay down the fears that held me back.

My Spirit was calling me to cease basing all my beliefs on negativity. My Spirit was calling me to trust in the unfailing and unconditional love of my Heavenly Father the way a child does. I was being challenged to once again believe in the wisdom of my heart.

This was truly the Family that would never forsake or let me down. This was the Family that would gladly supply all of my needs. This was the Family that would lead me to success.

Action

"We waste most of our time trying to get God to do something he has already done - or praying for God to do something He told us to do."

Jacquelyn K. Heasley

I remember the exact point when change literally began to occur overnight. It was late evening when tears began to pour. I was once again fighting my feelings of hopelessness. I begged for God to grant me a little mercy and bring an end to my endless unpredict-ability. I could take no more.

In spite of my tears, I went to bed giving thanks for my warm bed, the food that was in the pantry, and the fuel that had just been filled with my last remaining savings. I remember feeling a sense of peace as I dozed off to sleep.

Much to my surprise, I awoke the next morning to a call from my mother. She had just received a message from a man in Stamford who needed to get in touch with me immediately. He had misplaced my informa-tion and had been unable to reach me. He was insistent that I call him as soon as possible.

My conversation with him revealed God's interven-tion on my behalf. The lighting department where I long hoped to work was staying open and wanted to hire me on as manager. The executives would be com-ing in from Boston the next day to meet and iron out the details.

In an instant, my life took a 180-degree turn. My prayers were answered. It took all of my strength to hide my emotions and hold back tears of relief as I hung up the phone.

If I had chosen to give up and make decisions that answered the call of fear, I would have found myself achieving less favorable results. I would have taken a position offering lower pay. I would have been forced to begin work before I was able to make proper arrange-ments for the kids. I would have continued to struggle with my finances. I would have undoubtedly created a stressful environment for my family.

The timing in every aspect of the job offer was flawless. Because I allowed myself to be guided by my Spirit and hadn't taken a lesser job, I ended up making more money and having more freedom than expected. The necessary arrangements for my children's schooling had already been made. I knew without a doubt that I had followed in the exact direction God had laid out for me to travel. Because of this, I was able to receive His blessings in return.

Everything immediately fell into place. Looking back, I could see that allowing God's plan to unfold resulted in optimal results. There is nothing withheld from those of us who trust our Spirit and wait for God. If we are meant to have it, we will.

Ultimately, my faith directed my outcome. I placed my faith and attention on where I wanted to go, and I got there. If I had placed my faith and attention on where I did not want to go, I would have ended up with unfavorable results. The direction I traveled was based on the choices I had been willing to make.

Until we aim our faith in the direction God wants to take us and are willing to trust our Spirit to show the way, we will never be able to fully receive the provisions He has given us. We must start believing in the healing, loving, forgiving, uncontainable power of the Holy Spirit.

"Life isn't about finding yourself. Life is about creating yourself."
George Bernard Shaw

Chapter Six

STRUGGLES

"The harder the conflict, the more glorious the triumph. What we obtain too cheap, we esteem too lightly; it is dearness only that gives every-thing its value. I love the man that can smile in trouble, that can gather strength from distress, and grow brave by reflection. 'Tis the business of little minds to shrink; but he whose heart is firm, and whose conscience approves his con-duct, will pursue his principles unto death."

Thomas Payne

Life

"People are always blaming their circumstances for what they are. I don't believe in circumstances. The people who get on in this world are the people who get up and look for the circumstances they want, and if they can't find them, make them."

George Bernard Shaw

Fall had arrived with her endless array of New England colors. The autumn breeze cooled the air spreading the comforting smells of nature as she began to fall asleep. My dreams were becoming reality! The freedom I felt having my prayers answered was indescribable.

I put Kaden on the bus to school, left Anistyn with her new babysitter, and eagerly drove off to begin my first day on the job. My family would be financially secure. I would be able to stay in Connecticut. I was at peace.

My euphoria ended as quickly as it began. I recognized that my circumstances were less than ideal the moment I drove into the company parking lot.

My new place of employment was inconveniently located in the middle of an industrial park and resembled a dirty warehouse. This was hardly a location where customers would eagerly venture to purchase high-end home decorating items.

I couldn't believe my eyes as I walked through the front door and entered into a massive two-story entryway. I looked up to see unkept floor-to-ceiling windows. I looked down to find myself standing on dirty worn-out tile. Staring ahead, I saw white walls desperately in need of paint.

On a more positive note, the electrical counter just ahead was buzzing with life. The employees were too busy to notice me enter, so I decided to show myself upstairs to the showroom.

Halfway up, my heels caught in the uneven industrial grade vinyl covering the steps. Instinctively, my hands reached for the only available support, and I found myself clinging to a railing coated in a layer of black tarnish.

Once I regained my balance, I saw what was obviously meant to be the eye-catching focal point of the room—a massive chandelier hanging from the second-floor ceiling. Due to the cobwebs, dust, and years of neglect, the beauty of the piece was totally concealed.

Inside the showroom, I saw more of the same. Not one living being greeted me on the way in. The place looked and felt like a ghost town. Each wall was painted a different shade from the seventies: avocado green, purple, baby blue, mustard yellow, maroon, and something that resembled pink.

The employees' desks were mismatched damaged pieces of furniture situated towards the front of the building and sitting on a floor covered with unrecognizable stains.

I was staring at unsalable inventory. It was obvious that no new merchandise had been purchased in years.

The showroom literally consisted of dirty, out-of-date, overpriced chandeliers. Because of missing and broken light bulbs, the sales floor was a dark, musty, and uninviting place.

I thought my new job would be a challenge. I had no idea just how much I had underestimated the obstacle. The employees tried hard to do their jobs, but they had been left to manage by themselves for too long. Too many unproductive habits had been established. Business attire consisted of jeans and t-shirts. Customers were repeatedly ignored. Those who were helped often were not treated courteously.

It was imperative that I make drastic changes if there was to be any hope of this business getting back on its feet. I immediately implemented a more formal dress code, required tidy workstations, and insisted that customers be greeted at the door. My new demands encouraged all but one employee to find other work.

There was no time for training, so I was forced to navigate through a completely unfamiliar and complicated computer system while also making time to clean up the terrible mess left behind. Garbage filled desk drawers. Trash was left piled underneath. The desktops were cluttered with dirt, food, paper, and garbage. Filing cabinets were full of old job tickets. The bookshelves were overstocked with outdated sales material. The fluorescent fixtures had become a graveyard for insects. Gum remained a permanent addition to the chair cushions, and the computer keys would stick when used. I can truthfully say that the disorder was beyond anything I had ever seen.

I would soon learn that the lighting department had not always been run in this manner. The previous owner had, in fact, been very successful. At one time this business had a stellar reputation. I suppose that was the reason we still had what few customers we did. Unfortunately, the showroom's time-honored reputation was quickly becoming tarnished.

In hopes of turning things around, I did my best to put forward the most professional appearance possible. I would go to work every day wearing high heels, suits, and gloves. Here I was, dressed up in business attire, scrubbing on my hands and knees, attempting to produce an area fit to work.

There was never a time during the day for me to stop and take a break. When I wasn't taking care of customers, I was answering phones, pulling merchandise, or cleaning the showroom.

My only downtime was when I took a late lunch. At three o'clock each afternoon, I would run home, collect my son from the bus, and bring him back to the office to do his homework with me.

There was never enough time for me to meet the demands of each day. I had been given no formal training and was attempting to run a business with my hands tied behind my back. I had yet to be given the green light to hire new employees. And, if I had, I would have been completely unqualified to train them properly.

Every day seemed to put me deeper in the hole. I was too tired by day's end to give my children the care and attention they deserved. And, I can assure you, it didn't take long for my frustration to hit its peak.

Blame

"People spend too much time finding other people to blame, too much energy finding excuses for not being what they are capable of being, and not enough energy putting themselves on the line, growing out of the past, and getting on with their lives."

J. Michael Straczynski

*M*y discontentment with my situation was nonetheless justified. I had little salable inventory. The showroom was a mess. I was expected to do a job but had been given no means or support with which to do it.

I was walking a dangerous line. Finding a solution would be impossible if my focus remained on what was wrong with everything and everyone other than me. I would never overcome the problems until I was able to stop pointing fingers. It hardly seemed fair, but turning things around would only be possible by my taking full responsibility for the situation.

Fortunately, I had learned from past experiences that God always wanted me to succeed. I knew how valued I was as His creation. I never doubted that I was worthy of nothing less than the absolute best. Knowing this helped me see that I no longer needed to pass blame. Fault was meaningless. My best strategy was to learn how to make the most of other people's mistakes.

I resolved to move forward toward uncovering solutions. I had been hired to do a job that few would have been able to successfully undertake. Many were depending on my drive and determination to turn things around. These thoughts empowered me by helping me feel good about myself. Once I felt good, I began to work with more enthusiasm. My positive energy made it easier for me to finish out each day. Before I knew it, I was finding myself happy in spite of my troubles.

Perception

"Most folks are about as happy as they make up their minds to be."

Abraham Lincoln

No matter how much faith and positive thinking I put in, I often found myself beset by uninvited circumstances. Because I had no control over others, I had to face that I would never be able to fully govern my surroundings—not at work, not at home, and certainly not in relationships. If I didn't want to be manipulated by my circumstances, I had to find a way to pay better attention to how I chose to react.

But first I had to begin to appreciate each and every moment, to accept the good along with the bad. My contentment had nothing to do with my surroundings. It did, however, have everything to do with my approach to what was going on around me. Would I choose to see going home to pick up my child during my only break as a hassle, or could I recognize the blessing in having the freedom to take care of him in spite of my hectic schedule? Would I consider it a problem to ruin nice clothes cleaning a dirty showroom, or could I be blessed by the fact that I had been given the means to arrive at work professionally dressed? Would it be better to remain angry with employees for leaving, or could I be thankful for having the opportunity to hire a new staff of my choosing? If I chose my responses wisely, I felt I would move one step closer to happiness and success.

I began to see a solution in every situation. The question was how I would react to it. Once again, the aftereffects would ultimately be determined by my approach. If I chose a negative response, I would get a negative outcome. If I reacted in a positive manner, circumstances would undoubtedly change for the better.

Shortcomings

"Disability is a matter of perception. If you can do just one thing well, you're needed by someone."
Martina Navratilova

*N*ick Vujicic was born with no arms, no legs, only a small "chicken foot" as he calls it. Nick is able to get out of bed in the morning, turn on the lights, brush his teeth, shave, type on a computer, swim, play soccer, putt golf balls, prepare meals, and do most any other activity he sets his mind to.

What's more, Nick has traveled to fourteen different countries and encouraged more than two million people face-to-face. He lives his life by bringing happiness to others. Nick gives thanks to God every day for what he has, as well as for what he doesn't have. He teaches people to live a joyful life in spite of defeating conditions. By example, Nick courageously teaches how to avoid letting difficult circumstances stop anyone from overcoming challenges.

In describing his disabilities, Nick states, *"This is His (God's) love story for me; this is His love story of how much he loves me."* Nick knows and teaches that true happiness comes from changing the heart, not the circumstances. *"Sin, fear, and guilt are going to hold us back more than having no arms and legs will. These are the greatest disabilities of all. My circumstances don't need to change for me to be happy; I'm a miracle for somebody else."*

Many followers have blamed God for far less than what Nick has experienced. Here is my answer to why bad things seem to happen to good people: We have chosen to look past the blessing each situation holds.

This is why I like to see myself as a shell containing my Spirit. Without my Spirit, my body would be a helpless container. By choosing to live from my Heart as opposed to my head, I have the power to rise far beyond any restriction my body could ever encounter.

No one will ever be limited by intelligence, knowledge, education, finances, background, relationships, job, physical strength, or any other earthly restraint. In fact, there are no limits to what Spirit is able to accomplish. The truth of the matter is, in the end, nothing can stop our physical bodies from perishing. If we continue looking at our struggles from a negative perspective, our battles will never cease.

Be in the Moment

"Love the moment. Flowers grow out of dark moments. Therefore, each moment is vital. It affects the whole. Life is a succession of such moments and to live each, is to succeed."

Corita Kent

After Tommy's death, I was able to witness first-hand how the absolute worst life situations could be the opening to positive change. As I became willing to view things from this perspective, I could see that it would be impossible for me to reach my desired destination without first making it through the everyday bumps and bruises.

I couldn't be deceived and think God was not paying attention simply because things didn't run as planned. God's plan was always unfolding. **In my experience, suffering had been a side effect of seeing many of my prayers come to fruition.**

Suffering brought death to my old way of thinking. Pain caused me to want to change my way of living. Therefore, struggles didn't happen to me, they happened for me. I simply had to hold on to my faith during the process.

Each challenge was handing me the key to reaching a better tomorrow. Every moment was giving me an opportunity to decide my future. Choosing negativity would never lead to improved circumstances. Each choice I made was, in fact, an answer to this simple question: Would I be able to move forward in a productive fashion, or would I choose the negative and create more frustration?

I wanted to rest. I wanted comfort. I wanted my life to run smoothly. If I wanted to reach this place, I had to first allow my journey to recreate me. If I wanted to be patient, I first had to learn from experiencing situations that would give me the opportunity to practice patience. If I wanted to learn how to love unconditionally, I first had to experience situations where I would have to learn to tolerate intolerable people. If I wanted to be happy, I first had to learn how to find happiness in difficult times.

The starting point was allowing my quest to carry me through the healing process. I had to go through some pain to get past the negative effects that had been a result of my past choices.

But first I had to reach a place of acceptance. I had to take responsibility for what it was that was actually standing in my way. I was angry because I didn't want to be scrubbing the floors. I was afraid because I didn't feel I had the ability to turn things around. I was becoming bitter because I felt I deserved more training and support.

Accepting my current situation did not mean it was the best I could ever achieve. Once I was able to make the most of each situation, however, I was then better equipped to work my way through it.

Staying focused and present helped me to pinpoint what was truly standing in my way. My chaotic work environment and lack of training weren't really the problems at all. In fact, it was actually anger, bitterness, and feelings of hopelessness that were standing in my way of excellence. Once I was able to see the root of my troubles, I was then able to focus on allowing God to go to work healing the deeper issues.

Persistence

"Many of life's failures are people who had not realized how close they were to success when they gave up."

Thomas Edison

On close examination of any problem, I could easily picture a straight path from point A, my starting place, to point B, my desired outcome. The question was not where I wanted to go, however, it was how I could get there as quickly as possible.

To arrive anywhere in life requires dedication. That's why I would focus on putting into practice all that I knew while trusting that my dedication would produce my goal.

It sounded simple enough, but I still had trouble with diversions. Things such as lack of money, fatigue, frustration, and the simple lack of know-how kept getting in my way. As these issues came to the surface, I would find myself giving more of my attention to worrying about these concerns than I did trying to over-come them.

My desire to move quickly from point A to point B would be obscured when I came across an area in my life that I didn't necessarily want to address. In fact, most of the time I found myself trying to step around anything that made me uncomfortable.

I didn't like acknowledging that I was wrong in many instances—a diversion from learning humility. Oftentimes, I would rather stay angry as opposed to getting over myself—a diversion from learning uncon-ditional love and forgiveness. I didn't like that I had to spend much of my day doing things I didn't enjoy—a diversion from learning how to be a servant.

This is what I mean when I talk about diversions: I didn't want to stay on the road and work my way over the potholes. The more diversions I allowed, the more curves appeared in my road. The more turns, the longer the journey.

It was so common for me to avoid stepping over potholes that I hardly noticed myself doing it. I would allow anger to render me ineffective. I would put off doing unpleasant tasks. I would make excuses. Inevita-bly, I would find myself encountering the same prob-lem over and over again.

These diversions ultimately were leading me so far off course that I would find myself lost and confused. There were even times when I would take such a long detour that it would seem impossible for me to get back on track.

This would be most apparent when I would get my feelings hurt or feel that I had been taken for granted. I would focus so long on the pain of how others made me feel that I would eventually become too emotionally distraught to think clearly. Essentially, I was making life harder than it needed to be.

I became aware that many of my diversions were occurring because I was searching for solutions in the wrong places. Something as simple as a glass of wine at the end of the day would be relaxing, but it wouldn't diminish the cause of my stress. Yelling at my kids might allow me to release much of my frustration, but it did nothing to change the reason for my irritation.

Where we search for happiness is a sure-tell sign of where we believe happiness comes from. Obviously, happiness can't be found by searching in the wrong places. Sex, drugs, alcohol, money, relationships, and any other outside influences will never return authentic happiness. Most of the time, these are the causes of pain as opposed to the solutions. True healing will never be found by leaning on the very thing producing the pain.

Once I could see this, I quit wasting my time with the symptoms and got to work on dealing with the sickness. By dealing with the negativity, I began to notice the symptoms disappear on their own.

I had to be very mindful of what I asked for to help me find happiness. I didn't want to hinder my process by depending on anything that could destroy my life. If there was something I was dreading, I forced myself to do it. If my children needed attention, I dropped everything to spend time with them. If I was overstressed, I stayed home and got rest as opposed to spending a night on the town.

My persistence paid off because I did all I could to stay positive and avoid giving into fear and procrastination. I had allowed myself to pay attention to my needs and had met them by following the longing inside of me that lead to the most peaceful and loving solutions.

Healing

"We are all broken and wounded in this world. Some choose to grow strong at the broken places."
Harold J. Duarte-Bernhardt

I wish there existed wisdom where one could simply spout off a few magic words and cause grief to leave. Unfortunately, there is none that I know of. From my experience, the only way to go on is by actually doing it. Some days are worse than others.

Letting go of the old can be very difficult. First it takes tears, then bitterness, then anger, then confusion, and at times too much sorrow to bear. Experiencing these emotions is part of the healing process. If we choose, we can draw great strength from our pain. Pain heals us and teaches us. Pain is the door which can take each of us to a new life.

Most of us would go to any length to avoid experiencing heartache. Unfortunately, suffering is a fact of life that we will never fully escape. One cannot know a single component of any subject without also being aware of the opposite side. It stands to reason then that, without hardship, we would never fully know peace. One would not exist without the other. Our goal is not to eliminate suffering but to eliminate the negative outlook we possess of suffering.

I found the key to overcoming my struggles was to stop fighting every single area of my life all at once. A lot of what was going on around me was really an extension of a deeper issue.

My children would act out because I was coming home from work in a terrible mood. I was coming home in a terrible mood because I was overextending myself at work. I was overextending myself at work because I was unable to hire any help. I was unable to hire new employees because I was afraid to stand up to the corporate office and demand that I be given the tools and authority to run the business properly.

Once I identified the deepest underlying issue, I could finally see that much of the chaos I was experiencing had been a side effect of a single problem—fear. Fear was to blame for more than half of all my troubles. I was too concerned with trying to please others. I was too afraid of failure to take risks. I was too afraid of upsetting authority to stand up for what I believed needed to be done. Because I had begun to place my devotion outside of myself, I was unable to follow the Wisdom inside of me that was, in fact, trying to lead me to success.

I had begun reacting as opposed to acting. I was letting my circumstances control my behavior. I was creating much added suffering for myself by living on autopilot and not allowing my Spirit to help me in navigating through my life's struggles.

This led me back to the most basic message of all: I had to trust my Spirit. Suffering would cease to be hopeless once I stopped thinking with my head and listening to the positive voice of my Spirit. By making this adjustment, I would find myself no longer feeling helpless.

Suffering can only be overcome by restoration, and restoration comes from surrendering the body to Spirit and allowing Spirit to actively take the lead. When we continually fight our pain and struggle, we don't allow our bodies to heal and, therefore, our suffering continues.

I'll be the first to admit that sometimes I feel as if I'm being brought to the brink of despair. I feel as if my body can't possibly take any more. Some days I'm not sure I want to even get out of bed. At times like these, I have found that, by keeping in mind that this process is my Spirit's way of cleansing away the junk, I can acknowledge that the end is worth the means. Each day is bringing me closer to a brighter tomorrow.

"The perfect no-stress environment is the grave. When we change our perception, we gain control. The stress becomes a challenge, not a threat. When we commit to action, to actually doing something rather than feeling trapped by events, the stress in our life becomes manageable."

Greg Anderson

Chapter Seven

RELATIONSHIPS

"The bottom line is that people are never perfect, but love can be, that is the one and only way that the mediocre and vile can be transformed, and doing that makes it that. We waste time looking for the perfect lover, instead of creating the perfect love."

Thomas A. Kempis

Loneliness

"The person who tries to live alone will not succeed as a human being. His heart withers if it does not answer another heart. His mind shrinks away if he hears only the echoes of his own thoughts and finds no other inspiration."

Pearl S. Buck

I was beginning to clearly see that the way I chose to treat others and react to the way I was treated in return determined the outcome of my entire day. I had been giving unfriendly people power to ignite rage and frustration within me. My aggravation would quickly rise to the surface, and everyone in my vicinity would feel the effects.

At first, I believed the solution was to limit my interaction with people on an intimate level. Things were more peaceful for me emotionally when I stayed detached. I was happiest when things were simple and I could spend as much time as possible at home alone with my children.

Once again, I began to isolate myself. The fewer people I was forced to interact with, the less I had to worry about becoming hurt or frustrated. It was easier for me to live in peace when I didn't have to deal with inconsiderate persons getting in my way.

This was really just another way of me trying to control my surroundings. The real issue for me was not that most people were too difficult to tolerate. It was my having yet to learn how to avoid letting their actions and words affect me in a negative manner.

It didn't take long for me to conclude that keeping my distance was not the best way to remain peaceful. A better approach would be for me to give people around me the freedom to act and do as they may, while I, in turn, found a way to react to their actions that left me feeling uplifted. I had to uncover the means to do this regardless of how others might choose to treat me. It was the only way I could stop giving relationships the power to control my life.

To avoid getting worked up and bent out of shape, I had to see myself as an equal. I had to believe without question that not one person I came in contact with was better than me. Once I was able to see myself in this light, conflict and intimidation ceased to be a factor. I could walk away unstirred because I believed myself exceptional.

If I could learn to love myself completely and believe that I was worthy, I wouldn't have to worry about what others might be saying behind my back. If I could learn to be confident in my own beliefs and ideals, I wouldn't have to worry about disappointing anyone. If I could learn how to love people and accept them unconditionally, I wouldn't have to worry about their lack of acceptance hurting my feelings. It would no longer matter how I was treated if I could simply learn to consider myself exemplary despite others seeing me differently.

But I first had to do something that would have seemed a very selfish thing to do in the past. I had to put myself at the front of the line. I had to make taking care of myself a priority. I had to become my very own best friend—meaning, to be the faithful friend I could turn to get my needs met.

I had always been someone who did for others willingly. Somehow I had avoided seeing the importance in giving the best love and attention I was capable of giving back to me. In truth, if I didn't consider my own needs, I would never receive the best possible care. If I didn't fall passionately in love with myself, I would never know what it was to be a strong and courageous individual.

The idea of loving myself to the point where I could remain secure and happy while interacting with imperfect people seemed impossible. However, it stood to reason that if I was loved enough by myself, I would in turn become less affected by another person's lack of love. I could then remain happy despite how others reacted around me.

Individuality

"To go wrong in one's own way is better than to go right in someone else's."

Fyodor Dostoevsky

*B*efore I could confidently interact with others, I had to first know myself inside and out. So, I began taking note of my individual traits.

I began to see myself as someone who was blessed because I was able to see things differently. I was unique because I thought it more normal and productive to listen to my Spirit and allow myself to be guided to a solution rather than fight my way through it. I was honorable because I didn't feel a desire to get worked up by the petty gossip and backstabbing that seemed to be many people's favorite pastime. I was irresistible because I was someone who enjoyed looking for the beauty in everything and everyone around me. I was glorified because I liked trusting angels to direct me and help me navigate my day. I was dedicated because I refused to cheat not just on my husband, but on my hairdresser, doctor, and housekeeper as well. I was faithful because I put my family above all other relationships. I was appealing because I loved dressing up in nice clothes, while spending way too much money on haircuts, shoes, and handbags. I was a freethinker because I was able to love God and commit myself to leading a spiritually motivated life in spite of what others might think.

I was an absolutely unique individual. Once I sat back and looked at who I was, I discovered that I really liked the person in the mirror. Sure there were things I could do without, but nothing overshadowed my true essence. Seeing this helped me to begin to find peace with my exclusive individuality.

In fact, I truly loved myself. I honestly appreciated and respected the woman I had become. If I was going to let the real me shine forth, I could never try to be like someone else. I was born with my own set of goals and dreams. I believe with all my heart that I was placed on Earth to pursue a purpose. To live up to that calling, I first had to acknowledge the importance of not only avoiding judging humanity for their differences, but also accepting the differences within myself. Only by following my own inner calling would I ever become my optimal self.

I had been placing unnecessary weight on my shoulders by attempting to be someone I was not. Too many times I obsessed about wanting to look like a celebrity. Wanting to be the person who could make people laugh and turn any situation into a party was another fascination of mine. On another note, I made every attempt to judge myself by comparing my own possessions to others.

While one person's car would be better than mine, someone else would have a better sense of style. I wanted a supermodel's weight, height, and hair color. In the end, all I did was spend unnecessary time and money trying to turn myself into something I was never meant to be. Diet pills, designer clothes, and expensive cars never offered fulfillment. Trying to be someone else actually took away my happiness as opposed to adding to it.

It was only fitting that I wear the clothes I felt comfortable in. I needed to live where I felt was most beneficial for me. I shouldn't avoid pursuing relationships simply because I feared disapproval. It was okay to ignore the guest on "Oprah" who warned me not to go out in public without my makeup. Women's magazines were not the end all solution to learning the truth about a lady's body. It was perfectly acceptable to indulge my love for bargain shopping.

In a nutshell, I had to be willing to make a few mistakes and ruffle a few feathers by the simple fact that I was God's very own fingerprint in humanity. I was special and unique in my own way. The way I projected myself to the world needed to be a reflection of that very spectacular individual.

In allowing my own light to shine forth, I had to give myself the freedom to open up to a broader and different view on spirituality than that shared by most of my family and friends. While they had my best interest at heart, I had to be willing to trust my own instincts and walk away from teachings that weren't working.

Though I felt very alone at times pursuing my own vision, approaching life in my own way brought about new and improved results. I felt better about myself. I gained confidence. I began to attract healthier friendships. I became a much happier person. In truth, the best gift I ever gave myself was to step away from traditions and discover my own way.

Surroundings

"You are a product of your environment. So choose the environment that will best develop you toward your objective. Analyze your life in terms of its

environment. Are the things around you helping you
toward success – or are they holding you back?"

W. Clement Stone

I never wanted to be controlled by my surroundings. That being said, I couldn't help but acknowledge the strong role my living conditions played in determining whether I would experience a happy day. I needed a peaceful environment, and I set about to create it by concentrating on my home.

For my surroundings to offer me peace of mind and for my mood to improve, I had to have the house clean and orderly. It was imperative that I be out the door on time—without tripping over toys on my way to the car. Everything had to be nearly perfect: beds all made, grocery list updated to ensure properly stocked pantry, healthy lunches packed and ready to go, mail opened and bills paid, clothes in the dryer folded and put away, the rest of the laundry sorted in color-coordinated piles.

I was trying to find peace by attempting to maintain an immaculate home, successfully raise two kids, manage a struggling business, fit in five days a week of exercise, and get at least eight to nine hours of sleep at night.

I had so much to do that I never even considered time for myself. The problem was that I didn't know how to allow anything to be enough. Something could always be cleaned or organized. Laundry never ceased to grow. Food supplies always needed to be restocked. The kids would forever need to be in two different places at the same exact moment.

My nonstop activity wasn't helping me reach the end of my never ending to do list. I was going to have to come to terms with the fact that I would never be able to make peace with my surroundings.

My ability to maintain order was definitely a good thing. But none of it was worth the price of peace of mind. Finding peace meant making time to rejuvenate myself. That meant letting go of my desire to reach perfection and deciding that it was time to reevaluate any activity that didn't ultimately bring a healthy and self-loving feeling. I had to find other ways than cleanliness and orderliness to help me feel good about my surroundings.

This didn't mean I went the other extreme and decided to procrastinate and be lazy. The result of this behavior for me would be a lack of peace as well. When tasks are left undone and order is absent it is very difficult for me to relax. Knowing this, it became increasingly problematic for me to find the balance of living a productive life while refraining from overdoing it.

I started off by changing my environment from busy and loud to quiet and tranquil. I played soft, relaxing music. I allowed myself five-minute breaks to unwind with a cup of tea. I lit candles and dimmed the lights. I put on comfortable clothes and wore soft fuzzy socks. I found ways to surround myself with comfort. I discovered that once I was able to calm my surroundings, I was better able to calm myself.

Before, I considered beauty to be a spotless home and family to be a picture of perfection. Not only was the house spotless but the kids would be dressed to impress with groomed hair and matching shoes. There was a time when my home was adorned with pictures that were professionally taken. Without fail, everyone would be posed perfectly, wearing coordinating outfits while showing off bright smiles.

Recognizing that beauty is less of what is seen and more of the essence that lies within, I took down the posed shots and began to decorate with candid photos of my family and friends. I surrounded myself with authentic smiles, fun memories, and spontaneous expressions. Simply walking by a table would undoubtedly lift my spirits. A smile would never fail to appear on my own face each time I passed by my favorite memories.

I then went about hanging paintings on the walls that expressed my taste and personality even if they didn't match the décor. I took the formality out of my home by using soft paint, comfortable furniture, and anything else that would relax me. I made sure that everything went together and looked pretty without having to spend a lot of money redecorating. I simply made my home a reflection of me. These meaningful changes helped me to see the essence of the beauty surrounding me.

I did anything I could to make my environment an escape from stress as opposed to being the cause of it. Unfortunately, this meant continuing to wipe off the dust, clean the floors, and wash the windows. However, I didn't kill myself trying to get it all done at once.

Clutter was another thing interfering with my stability and happiness. Although I dreaded the task of clearing out the junk, surprisingly I found it to be a very therapeutic process. I was amazed to find that moving out the excess actually helped relieve stress.

The task of releasing all the unneeded things in my environment was monumental in helping to lighten my load. Clothes were easier to put away. I never had trouble finding what I was looking for. Better yet, my cleaning ritual was practically cut in half.

Getting outside is still another way I find for building healthy relationships. I made time to sit on my deck, lie on the grass in my backyard, or simply take a walk around the block. The strength and calm I find in nature is an invaluable gift for my soul.

I focus on the sky, the formation of the clouds, the color of the leaves, the effortless flight of birds, the warmth of the sun on my face. Slipping into the outdoors provides a break from my endless reasoning. Nature walks slow down the speed of my thoughts and help me to acknowledge the beauty of the present moment. Nature offers me much-needed medication for relaxation, stress reduction, and mental restoration.

Connection

"When a hundred men stand together, each of them loses his mind and gets another one."

Friedrich Nietzsche

J felt so confident in myself that my need to condemn others began to disappear. I didn't care if a person was straight, gay, bisexual, or transsexual. I could just as easily talk to a Democrat as I could a Republican, Liberal, or an Undecided. I enjoyed being around blue collar workers just as much as I did the wealthy Wall Street stock brokers. Tattoos, multiple piercings, and funky colored hair intrigued me more than triggered my disapproval.

Once I stopped making judgments, I was better able to recognize the love and beauty within most beings—I say most because, let's face it, I'm still human—and my self-assurance began to really stand out. The more I fell in love with myself, the less I cared about how others chose to live their lives.

It wasn't that I had become overconfident and arrogant. I simply felt really good about the woman I was learning how to be. I never saw myself as superior. I had no egotistical feeling whatsoever. I simply knew I was worthy of belonging.

I was an asset to others as opposed to being the one draining the life out of everyone. I was happy. I loved to be around people and made an effort not to interfere. I was easy to please and able to go with the flow. Because my actions ceased to inconvenience others, I began to attract healthy connections.

This is when I began to think about how one person's behavior has the power to affect all of humanity. I pictured each of us as a tiny drop in an enormous mass of water. One single drop, me, would be helpless if it chose to stand alone.

On its own, a tiny drop of water is completely ineffective. No matter how pure the substance, there isn't enough of it to sustain any kind of life. Without connections, a single drop is absolutely powerless, isolated, ineffective, and eventually dries up. The only way for a water drop to be anything significant is to connect to more of its own.

Gather enough raindrops, get them moving together, and wonders will take place. Nothing will ever be able to stop the power of the sea, for example. All the drops of water in the sea, working as a unified body, will eventually have the strength to move mountains, topple cities, and nourish the earth.

This proves how important it is for me to take responsibility for my behavior. As we begin to connect to one another, we also begin to move as one. In the end, my actions ultimately affect and dictate the quality of another's life.

I could help someone improve their day, or I could make things more difficult for them. I could let someone back into a line of traffic, or I could let them sit there and wait it out. I could help a total stranger feel noticed by saying hello, or I could hold my head down and ignore anyone I didn't know. I could do my best to remember names, shake hands freely, and offer hugs, or I could step back and maintain my distance.

All of these acts seem small and insignificant, but I can assure you that they are significant to the person on the receiving end. Every little act makes a difference. Each one of us can reduce negativity by simply choosing to be kind and courteous.

It wasn't good enough that I had learned how to love myself. It was just as important for me to learn how to love everyone around me. Before, I really didn't understand the concept of unity. I didn't like the idea of connection.

Because I had experienced the pain of having others lie, cheat, and take advantage of me, it was very difficult for me to trust anyone now. I didn't see the benefit in trying to function for the greater good of the whole. It seemed much safer to stand alone so I could better manage the direction of my own destiny.

It was apparent to me that this was the mentality of the greatest number of people. However, I was not interested in settling for living the type of life that most people ended up living. Those mainly interested in knocking people down are the ones who eventually end up being the ones to fall the hardest. They have surrounded themselves with superficial communities. The people they have connected with are only joining in because it suits their own interests in return. Where there is selfishness, there is no trust. Where there is no trust, there is no stability.

People are attracted to the shining light of kindness the way a moth is to a flame. A community growing from the basis of love and consideration is stable. Once people feel loved, they are then able to give it more freely. Simple acts of kindness form circles of generosity that become unstoppable.

I didn't want to end up as one of those people who only give or help others as long as there is something to gain in return. My life was not going to be about what others could do for me. It was going to be about how I could exemplify the positive feelings I carried around inside of me. If I could help a total stranger feel even the slightest amount of the love I felt, then any small act of kindness would be worth the effort.

I might not be savvy enough to keep from getting taken advantage of. It may be nearly impossible for me to know who's telling the truth. However, I have a habit of trusting in a Power greater than man. This Greater Power is constantly focused on helping me. I have no doubt that He is perfectly willing and able to keep me from being tossed around by the harmful waves collective humanity might create.

I would never be able to receive anything of value if I wasn't willing to first give it away. Joy comes from giving. Abundance comes from giving. Safe and happy connections are established by giving. To be truly happy, one must first be willing to circulate a little happiness around. We do that by connecting to those around us, offering love and kindness along the way.

Career

"To succeed you need to find something to hold on to, something to motivate you, something to inspire you."

Tony Dorsett

When I first came to Connecticut and began my new job, I was determined to look good, find favor, and become a productive manager. My sole ambition was to make money and find success.

I quickly discovered how unfulfilling it was to simply focus on promoting myself. I was much happier when I aimed my energy at being of service. That's when my vision regarding my career changed from building a successful company to creating a kind and loving environment where customers could get the help they needed. I became more interested in finding out how I could be of help and less preoccupied with how I could make the biggest profit. Pushy sales tactics gave way to courteous and respectful guidance.

Now that I had been given the okay to hire new staff, I began to look for the same helpful qualities in my prospective employees as well. Because my focus was on kindness, I was able to recognize kindness in others. I passed over very qualified candidates in favor of some with less experience, using my Intuition to find the most effective employees. In the end, I surrounded myself with people who were passionate, dedicated, driven, and interested in meeting the needs of the company rather than fulfilling their own agendas.

I knew in my heart that prosperity would follow any venture I undertook as long as my focus was less on what was in it for me and more on how I could meet the needs of others. Ultimately, my needs would be met regardless of the amount of money I made.

Because I had always found money and work to be unstable and unpredictable, I didn't rely on either to be the solution to my every problem. I no longer viewed work as determining whether or not I would be a success. Work was an important tool, but it was not the only one available in my box. My job was not my actual Provider. My paycheck was necessary, but I knew God's provisions were not limited to my salary. As long as I focused my best effort on being exceptional in unselfish ways, I knew I had nothing to fear.

Race

"Give love and unconditional acceptance to those you encounter, and notice what happens."
Wayne Dyer

I mentioned earlier how quickly day care facilities fill up in the area where I live. Some parents place their child on a day care wait list as soon as he or she is born! After Anistyn's baby sitter resigned, I faced major challenges in the system.

Hoping to keep Anistyn in as intimate an environment as possible, I began doing research on reputable in-home child care. Because she had already undergone such drastic change, I didn't feel comfortable placing her with the typical nine-to-five structured institution. I was fortunate indeed to come across two locations with available space due to last-minute cancellations.

I was very impressed with the first option. I pulled up to a beautifully manicured yard surrounded by a white picket fence. The freshly painted home with its beautiful assortment of blooming flowers looked like something straight off a movie set. Inside was just as eloquent. The home was absolutely spotless. The chil-

dren had an indoor fenced-in play land set aside specifically for their use.

It appeared to be the perfect place for a two-year-
old to spend her days. I almost signed the contract on
the spot, but something kept telling me to wait until I
had a chance to view all my options.

The second house was a bit older than the first.
The yard was kept, but I was caught off guard by
the run-down car blocking the driveway. I was met at
the door by an older and extremely frazzled woman
named Miss Betty. Though she had much kindness in
her eyes, she looked like the kids had begun taking a
toll on her.

The hinges on the screen door squeaked as she let me
inside, where I witnessed a bit of a mess and a lot of com-
motion. The house wasn't dirty, but toys were everywhere.
The carpet was a little worn down and spotted with Kool-
Aid stains. The kids had complete access to the home and
were constantly moving from the living room down to the
basement and back up again. They had dirt on their hands
and food on their faces. Beyond this, what stood out to me
the most was the fact that Miss Betty, along with each and
every child in her care, was black.

Miss Betty had the kids run outside to play so we
could have a moment of silence. She impressed me by
not feeling a need to apologize for the noise—or the
mess. She quickly informed me we were limited on
time because the kids would be getting hungry soon.

I left our meeting feeling as if I had little to consider. Sending Anistyn to the first location seemed the
only logical conclusion. That's when an eye-opening

question popped into my head: If every child at Miss Betty's was white, would I be willing to give a little more consideration to sending Anistyn to her school?

The first day care looked great on the outside. The children had plenty to keep them busy throughout the day, and I liked that their area was clean and well-organized. However, the price was a bit out of my range, and the location was not convenient. I would be adding an extra forty minutes to my daily commute once I factored in the long traffic. I hadn't seen the kids in action very long, but I witnessed enough to see that their activities were very structured. It was obvious to me that discipline and order were high priorities.

Anistyn, on the other hand, is the type of child to do best with fewer restrictions and more freedom. She is very sensitive and needs a lot of affection and personal attention.

The reality was that my daughter would do better in the home environment of Miss Betty's school. I loved that Miss Betty's home appeared a bit chaotic. When kids are happy and having fun, things tend to be a little out of order. She expected the children to be loud and messy. I could see that scattered toys throughout her house were a natural and welcomed part of the children's day. I appreciated the way Miss Betty didn't make excuses. I respected her honesty and ability to let the kids be authentic. It was that obvious that her entire life had been given over to the kids in her care. As an added bonus, the price of her school was within my budget. Another plus was the fact that I could take back roads and make it to Betty's in five minutes.

My only real concern was Anistyn being the only white child in an all-black day care. I realized that this was a problem with my way of thinking. It had nothing to do with the quality of care the school would provide for my daughter.

The following week, I walked Anistyn through the front door of her new afternoon home. She instantly received the biggest open-armed hugs from screaming kids who were excited to meet their new friend. Anistyn's skin color didn't matter to her or them. She was immediately accepted and loved.

Anistyn was automatically treated like everyone else. Every day I dropped her off dressed to the nines. I would have her angelic little face clean, her long golden blonde hair brushed and styled to perfection, and her clothes pressed and strategically matched.

Each day I picked her up, I would find her wearing mismatched clothes and sporting multiple braids or an assortment of pony tails. Miss Betty wouldn't listen to my explanation that white girl's hair wasn't supposed to be styled that way. She would dismiss me by letting me know that she did all the girls' hair that way. Anistyn was not to be left out. If a little blonde white girl wanted her hair to look like the other kids, she would be happily obliged by Miss Betty.

Needless to say, I would get plenty of odd looks any time I ran errands after picking her up from daycare. It became a pattern for the grocery store clerks to look for us just to see how she would appear next.

Anistyn never questioned whether she belonged with all the other children. She knew she was loved. Yes, the kids ran around with dirty faces, but not because they weren't cared for properly—because they were having too much fun to stay clean.

Outer appearances can be so deceiving. I never again wanted to sell myself short by making judgments due to the color of one's skin, education, income level, the size of someone's home, or the clothes they wore.

I made the best choices by digging a bit deeper to see the true qualities of a person's heart. Love, kindness, and the ability to give and receive are far better judges of character than first impressions. There was never a better example of this than the relationship I established with my beloved Miss Betty.

My daughter belonged to this woman during the day. If I was late, it was overlooked. If I needed to get to work early, the door would be open and a bed ready to lay her back down.

If Betty's dark skin, squeaky door, or messy home had been the determining factor in my decision, I would have made the wrong choice concerning my daughter's care. Thank goodness I was given the eyes to see past my own ignorance. This place was where my daughter was meant to be. She was happy and looked forward to going to school each day. Miss Betty provided her not with a day care, but with a home.

Religion

"Keep in mind that our community is not composed of those who are already saints, but of those who are trying to become saints. Therefore let us be extremely patient with each other's faults and failures."

Mother Teresa

*M*y son was having a difficult time with the move. I had taken him away from everything that brought him a sense of safety and love. Not only did we have to leave his beloved dog behind, but he missed his grandparents, aunts, uncles, and friends tremendously.

Our Texas neighborhood was a place where Kaden could play outside from morning until night. There were kids of all ages living in almost every house. The cul-de-sac at the end of our street was home to endless basketball games. Driveways were transformed into parking lots for bicycles the instant kids were released from school. Concrete chalk was the welcomed graffiti adorning the sidewalks. Normal for Kaden meant having endless playtime with a continual supply of friends.

In our new Connecticut neighborhood, there were no sidewalks, and the streets weren't a safe place for youngsters to play by themselves. Most kids stayed home and played in their own backyards.

Random playtime and open front doors were no longer a way of life. I quickly learned that if children wanted to get together, parents first scheduled playdates. I had never even heard the word "playdate" before. And, unfortunately, I couldn't make dates for my child because I had yet to meet any families myself. It was all very frustrating for my son.

Kaden took matters into his own hands. He had seen two boys, a redhead and a blonde, whom he thought might live up the street. Kaden never saw them together, but he was convinced they were brothers because they both seemed to appear from the same house.

I encouraged him to go up to the top of the hill and introduce himself. After a few days of working himself up to the task, Kaden finally found the will to knock on their front door. This was when my son first met the family that quickly began filling the void in his heart.

Zack, the blonde, was very athletic. Soccer was his chosen sport, but anything involving running shoes and balls would do. On the other hand, the redhead, named Aaron, was studious, quiet, and seldom allowed his attention to wander far from his latest book. Aaron much preferred going to the library to kicking around a silly ball. Reading for entertainment never even crossed his brother's mind. The boys had nothing in common; the fact that they were twins was almost impossible to conceive.

Kaden was an interesting component to add to this combination. He loves sports and could occupy Zack's need for physical entertainment, but he's also very smart and takes pride in learning. This meant Aaron had someone who could relate to him as well. Needless to say, the twins, who were growing up with little interaction before, found common ground in the one friend they were able to share—my son.

Kaden quickly became the third child in the Bayles home. He went there immediately after school and stayed until I forced him to come home. Rob and Sheri, the boys' parents, made sure Kaden ate a healthy snack and helped him finish his homework. Once the weekend arrived, finding one of the boys alone was impossible.

I was quickly brought under the Bayles' roof as well. Sheri would keep Kaden for me on snow days when the kids weren't able to attend school. She was always available to listen to my tales of frustration and to help me navigate the difficult path of raising children alone. I was a terrible cook, but delicious homemade meals were available any time we were willing to hike up the hill for dinner.

Eventually, my children and I were invited to join the Bayles for holiday celebrations as well. Interestingly, while my children and I celebrate Christian holidays, the Bayles family observes the Jewish calendar.

Regardless of our differences, Kaden began spending every Friday night with the twins celebrating Shabbat. His favorite meals soon consisted of roasted chicken and other foods I had never heard of, matzo balls and challah being the main two. He enjoyed going with the boys to temple and respectfully wore a borrowed yarmulke. He even attended Hebrew school a time or two. He couldn't understand a word spoken in class, but everyone made him feel welcome despite his nonexistent knowledge of Hebrew.

I crossed paths with very few Jewish people while living in the South, so I was completely unfamiliar with their customs and beliefs. I honestly thought kosher was simply a brand of pickles. During our first Hanukkah celebration, I naively asked Sheri what the foil in the menorah symbolized. She laughed while putting her arms around me to explain it was just to keep the candles from falling over!

If I had been unwilling to accept the customs and religion of others, I would have missed out on bonding so closely with this beloved family. Our willingness to accept and respect one another opened the doors to a unique and warm friendship.

Our relationship with the Bayles family grew to go far beyond friendship. My son had the privilege of performing the best friend speech at the twins' bar mitzvah, while my family was given the proud honor of lighting one of the thirteen candles on their birthday cake.

It was at this time that I began to relax my views on religion. In the past, I had a very rigid way of thinking, and my unwillingness to examine other points of view caused me to be very narrow-minded. In truth, the more content I became with my own relationship with God, the more able I was to see our equality with people of other persuasions. A person's chosen beliefs, whether it be their sexual orientation, political viewpoint, religion, or any other difference of opinion became a minor topic.

More often than not, I formed my greatest friendships with people I would have chosen to avoid in my previous life. Quite frankly, those who think and act very differently than I do have turned out to be some of my favorite companions.

What became clear to me is that God's love is too infinite to leave anyone behind. We are all loved and valued unconditionally by Him. I found freedom in recognizing that it was not merely okay but healthy for me to welcome diversity.

What I valued most from my wonderful relationship with Rob, Sheri, and the twins was my newfound awareness that I never again wanted to use religious differences as barriers. I began to view religion as a path to Love as opposed to a separation tactic—a path with many different byways to reach our final destination.

I now love to see—and I greatly admire—the ways in which varied people express their love for God. I have chosen to see every person as neither right nor wrong, but simply unique in his or her own right.

Parting

"Above all, be true to yourself, and if you cannot put your heart in it, take yourself out of it."

Hardy D. Jackson

As I stated earlier, one of the reasons I chose to move to Connecticut was because of my close relationship with Travis. He was living up North now so that he could be closer to his daughter, who was living in Connecticut with his former wife.

While I was still living in Texas, Travis never forgot about me. Despite his demanding job and many personal responsibilities, he continued to call and check on me every day. Travis stayed by my side and tried to ease my desperation at a time when most of my other friends chose to take to the sidelines.

Our friendship blossomed into a very genuine and caring love relationship, one that helped push me toward moving. I felt very fortunate to find myself loved and adored by the man who had now become my best friend in the world. I had been vulnerable, and he had been willing to help pick up the pieces. I had been lonely, and he had been there to hold me. I had been lost, and he was there to remind me who I was.

After Tommy's death, Travis made it his mission to make me happy. Our sharing and supporting one another through such deep sorrow formed an unbreakable bond between us. He was determined to shield me from further heartbreak, becoming someone I could truly depend on. It was no secret that I loved him dearly.

After my move to Connecticut, Travis had become my rock. Not only did he cook, clean, and work in the yard, he did everything he could for the kids as well. If I couldn't make it home in time to get Kaden to football practice, Travis would leave work early and take my son wherever he needed to go. If Anistyn didn't feel well, Travis and I would rotate days off work to stay home with her. We had become a team. There was no doubting his love for me and the children.

Travis never pushed me to give more of myself than I was able to give, but in spite of that, I still wasn't happy. Maybe I wasn't able to give my whole heart to Travis because most of it still belonged to Tommy. Maybe my wounds had been so deep that true intimacy simply wasn't possible anymore. Maybe I was too confused to appreciate all that I had to be thankful for. Maybe I would never be able to be happy with anyone else again. I was conflicted in so many ways, but I knew for certain that I wanted to move on with my life. I was determined to fight my unhappiness.

Travis made many sacrifices for me and the children. Though our old friends didn't approve of our being together, he stayed by me nonetheless. He was there to help me move; he was here now to help me maintain my new home. He took on the role of fathering my children with ease, and they loved him as much as he loved them.

I couldn't bear to lose the one person in my life that I could truly count on. I desperately tried to force my heart to line up with my head. I didn't want my children to be cut off from yet another valued relationship. Most of all, I felt guilty and didn't want to hurt this truly spectacular man.

I fought my knowing that this relationship wasn't right for me and went along as if everything was fine. We moved in together. I tried to spend more time with him, even taking weekend vacations. Nothing worked. It seemed that the more I tried to make something happen, the more certain I became that it never would.

We could easily step into the role of family if I would just let the relationship be. But something didn't feel right. The thought of losing Travis made me sick, but the idea of staying together left me feeling incomplete. In reality, the longer I tried to make things work and the harder I pushed to keep us together, the worse I felt.

I carried the turmoil for months knowing that my unease was not going away. Despite loving Travis and wanting to be with him, I knew I had to let him go. It was difficult getting my head to line up with the rest of me. I was afraid of hurting my children. I was afraid of losing a friend. I was afraid I wouldn't be able to make things work on my own. Most of all, I was afraid of hurting someone I loved.

In the end, the love I felt for myself won out. It was simply impossible for me to settle for anything that wasn't working to my benefit. None of my fears proved worthy enough reasons for me to hold on. There was no doubt in my mind that Travis and I were meant to be together for a time. But, I could now see that we were not destined to be together for a lifetime.

I was gambling with the happiness of everyone involved by ignoring my instincts and trying to hold on to a relationship that had run its course. I believe that God puts people in our path to help us along the way. I was there for Travis just as much as he had been there for me. Just because we love people doesn't mean they are to remain a permanent part of our lives. Some friendships, even good ones, are simply not meant to last.

I put aside my fear and guilt and broke off our relationship. As I suspected, the news did not go well. Travis had given up a great deal, including his home and friends, to make things work with me. He accepted my children and loved and cared for me unconditionally. He was losing everything through no fault of his own. He couldn't understand why I was doing this, and I couldn't find the right words to explain the reasons myself.

He shielded himself by becoming cold and distant. He walked out of my life, refusing to look back. From that day on, I had no idea where he moved or whom he was spending his time. We were no longer a part of each other's lives.

Despite being heartbroken by this loss, I knew I made the right choice. Beneath the pain and sadness, I felt as if a weight had been lifted. I was content.

My children seemed to take this in stride. Anistyn was too young to really question what was going on. Kaden said that if Travis wanted to walk away from him just because things didn't work out with me, then Travis didn't really love him in the first place. I didn't necessarily agree with my son, but I was proud that he was not blaming himself.

I knew that all of us would benefit in the long run. God's solutions are good for everyone involved, whether we see that right away or not. There was more going on than a simple breakup. I had turned my life over to a Divine Power. This Power was still in the midst of completing an amazing transformation in my life. My pain would only be temporary as long as I stayed determined to follow my heart.

I accepted our fate as part of a growing process for us both. This meant allowing Travis to experience his own grief and react in his own way. I could not try to fix him or ease his pain. I had to trust that God could handle everyone involved far better than I ever could. Interfering would only hinder us in the long run. Unfortunately, in doing so, I lost one of my most valued companions.

Love

"The moments of happiness we enjoy take us by surprise. It is not that we seize them, but that they seize us."

Ashley Montagu

I was coming to find that Stamford was a very tight knit community. One would think a city of this size would breed strangers. This was far from true. I came to find out, the city of Stamford was much like the small town I grew up in. Seems private matters weren't so private after all. My many hours of working near a supply house taught me that men gossip just as much as the ladies do. Sooner or later, I heard a little negativity about everyone.

To my surprise, there was one man whose reputation seemed to stand out from the crowd. His name was Rick, a Stamford citizen born and raised. He owned a successful electrical company in town, which had him coming to the electrical supply from open until close. He held his employees to high standards, and they remained loyal to him for years. His crew was clean-cut and easily recognizable due to the fact that their shirts were matching and always neatly tucked into their jeans. His trucks were well-maintained and he had a reputation for leaving a job in better condition than he found it.

During a discussion with the guys at work, I learned that Rick had taken notice of me months ago. I also found out how disappointed he had been to discover I was unavailable. Seeing the recent change in my relationship status, the guys felt it was their duty to arrange another introduction.

I had no intention of letting this idea go any further than talk. Rick was a valued customer of my company, though not a part of the business I managed. Getting involved with a customer was not a good idea. Regardless, I couldn't help notice that nothing but kind words were ever spoken when Rick's name came up in conversation. Even his competitors were fond of him.

Still, I was enjoying the freedom of having no strings attached. I liked the idea of maintaining some control over my life. I enjoyed the simplicity of spending time alone. Dating would only complicate matters.

Everyone at the office seemed to think I should consider the idea of getting to know Rick better. It began to feel like a conspiracy. Any time I came down to the counter, conversation inevitably led to this esteemed customer.

The general consensus was that, on a scale from one to ten, Rick was a fifteen. I heard how he was the nicest guy anyone had ever met, how he would give a stranger the shirt off his back, how he wired someone's house for free. I was told that Rick loved kids, despite having none of his own, and that he even coached little league hockey. A local police officer informed me that Rick was the best guy in town. With a smirk, he said that this hadn't always been the case, but those were stories for another time. For now, all I needed to know was that a girl couldn't do better.

One afternoon the manager of the electrical counter, a man I had grown to love and respect tremendously, came upstairs to go over some paperwork in my office. He seemed to be the only one refraining from discussing my personal life. I couldn't help but ask him what he thought about my dating one of his customers.

He looked me square in the eyes and said, "Kerie, you're a good girl. You've been through a lot. I just want you to be happy." When I asked what he would do if Rick asked his daughter out, he responded by telling me he could only wish Rick would ask his daughter out. Immediately following our conversation, I went downstairs and told the guys to set us up.

Poor Rick. He was completely caught off guard—he had no idea people had been attempting to hook us up. I don't know if he was more surprised or embarrassed. Regardless, he handled the situation with grace. Before the day's end, he was knocking on the door to my office asking if he could introduce himself.

Rick's demeanor was quite cute if you ask me. He looked ready to be anywhere but standing in front of me. I couldn't help but notice the way his baby blue eyes stood out against his dark skin and jet black hair. He was confident yet a little reserved—and very sweet. He didn't stay long, just long enough to say hello and to let me know he looked forward to our date that weekend.

Another couple who happened to be mutual friends agreed it would be less awkward if they double-dated with us. The four of us enjoyed a nice evening out in Manhattan. During dinner, I was surprised by Rick's playful nature and confidence. I was further impressed when he worked to help the waiter clear off the table.

Following dinner, we went down the street to a small tavern. Rick was the life of the party, not only in our own little crowd, but among the strangers standing around us as well. My date befriended just about anyone. His big smile never left his face, and his laugh was infectious. He was comfortable to spend time with. Rick didn't crowd over me, but was mindful to ensure that I was having a good time. He enjoyed buying drinks and was back and forth delivering refills better than the wait staff. He didn't appear to be trying to impress me with his behavior. He simply seemed to enjoy doing nice things for those around him.

Rick and I talked about work and life in New England. I realized he knew nothing about me whatsoever. It was refreshing to be in the company of someone who wasn't feeling pity. I didn't want to focus on my past, and he didn't push. Instead, he tried to find out how well I was adjusting to moving from Texas.

He could see that I was having a little trouble and responded by letting me know that he would be around to help with my yard and getting the house ready for winter. He would come out with his crew next week to make sure everything was in order. He didn't argue but simply ignored me when I let him know that was not necessary.

As the night began to wear down, the four of us headed back to Connecticut. The plan was to drop me off with Rick and let him give me a ride home from his apartment. That's when my impression began to waver. If I had been operating under some misconception that this man was perfect, I was quickly brought back to reality by the condition of his home.

When we went upstairs to get his keys, I found myself standing in the doorway of a five hundred square-foot disaster. I don't know how on earth a bed, kitchen, bathroom, and living area could fit in such a small space. And I could hardly see beyond the mess. I definitely had some thinking to do. Rick's nature appeared to be the complete opposite of my clean and orderly one. I thought the showroom at work was bad when I arrived. This was definitely running a close second.

The kitchen counter was hidden under a week's worth of unopened mail. The floor was covered in clothes. The floor tiles had broken loose to expose the concrete slab. The couch was home to hockey bags, ice skates, and baseball equipment. The dresser drawers were falling out of the chest, and the closets didn't close due to their overflowing contents. The only place that was neat was the bed, which was carefully made.

After Rick found his keys we walked downstairs to an underground garage. Lo and behold, a black two-seater Corvette would be my ride home. As he opened the car door, I could tell he cared more about the Corvette than he did about any other possession. The vehicle was in absolute mint condition. It had definitely received the white-glove treatment—there were no streaks on the windows, no dirt on the floors, and not a single spot on the freshly washed paint.

I had no question that Rick was a kind and good-hearted man, but from what I could see, he might need to rethink his priorities. I had been on only one date, but after Tommy, I didn't want to take even the slightest chance on falling for someone who wouldn't make a good all-around companion.

During the ride home, Rick asked me about my children and said he sincerely hoped to meet them soon. He wanted to know their ages, grade levels, if they played sports, what their hobbies were, the color of their hair and eyes, and how they were adjusting to life away from Texas.

He surprised me by drilling me about my choice of babysitter. He knew I was new in town and wondered how I found her, how much I knew about her, if I did a background check; was she okay staying with the kids this late, how old she was, and did the kids mind being left with her?

Once we arrived, Rick wanted to know how much babysitters made these days and handed me the money to pay for my sitter without a second thought. I wouldn't accept of course, but that one act helped me forgive the messy state of his apartment.

Rick was the biggest walking contradiction I had ever seen. His home reminded me of a carefree bachelor's pad. His car said flashy and a little wild. His work told me he was loyal, dependable, and hardworking. His giving nature spoke of kindness and love. In the end, I didn't know what to think of Rick whatsoever.

I lay in bed that night confused. It seemed funny to even care after only one date, but something told me that if I decided to move ahead with this man, there would be no turning back.

The next morning I couldn't help think about Miss Betty and the Bayles family and reminded myself how much I could miss by letting first impressions and differences dissuade me. There was much more to Rick than a messy apartment and a fast car. For starters, he always looked after the needs of others. He gladly paid for dinner, bought drinks, offered to drive, and cleaned up after everyone. He was widely respected in the community. Rick was no stranger to working twenty-hour days, then using the money to help someone in need. The man was simply unlike anyone I had ever met.

The following day, I found Rick standing at my front door. I didn't expect to hear from him again so soon, let alone have him contact me in person. Then again, nothing about Rick had been typical. I let him into the house, and we walked into the kitchen. I tried to figure out whether to let myself feel the excitement bubbling up or whether to put an end to this now. Rick waited for neither. He simply waited for me to turn around and gave me a kiss.

Settling In

"May the love hidden deep inside your heart find the love waiting in your dreams. May the laughter that

you find in your tomorrow wipe away the pain you find in your yesterdays."

Anonymous

*T*his was just before Thanksgiving. We saw each other every day from that moment until we were separated by our Christmas vacations. Once I got past the messy apartment and flashy car, I could see that Rick was indeed an absolute perfect fit for me. We were amazing together. We shared the same values. He was kind and considerate to my children. It was comical to watch him try to teach Kaden to skate and play hockey while never letting Anistyn out of his sight.

The children and I never went without. Thankfully, Rick's second car was a Jeep Cherokee. He was able to pick the kids up in case I needed to work late. We were taken out to dinner three to four times a week. If we stayed in, Rick would have pizza in one hand and a bottle of Coke in the other. I could count on at least one night a week being set aside for just the two of us, but the rest of the time Rick was adamant that we include the kids in our activities.

We had a great time going to Rick's hockey and baseball games. He would playfully attract Anistyn's attention while he stood on third base or wave us down in a silly way while skating on the ice. Any time we planned to be in the stands, Rick made sure people would find and include us in their group. We were never strangers. His friends welcomed us with open arms. I went from being an isolated new member of society to having countless people to turn to any time I needed help.

Once Rick discovered I was looking for a good hairdresser, he got me an appointment with the best in town. I was having trouble finding a pediatrician who accepted new patients, but with one call, I had an appointment set the next day. If I needed a plumber, one was ready to help me out. When my car had a problem, it was towed and fixed before I knew it was gone. I even had a limo service paid for and at my door to take us to the airport once Rick realized he wouldn't be able to drive us himself.

Rick gave to the community, and the community was happy to give back to him. Anything someone would do for him, they would also do for me and my children. Rick took on any burden to ensure that I had no worries to speak of. He even came by to take care of my trash so I didn't have to pay a company to do it.

I never before experienced the fairy-tale life this man was now offering. People don't just sweep you off your feet and take care of you. It was so foreign to feel safe. It was such a shock to experience devotion.

After my experience with Tommy and most of my past relationships, I was finding it hard to trust in love and companionship. I came out of a world where nothing was ever certain and where my circumstances were shaky and undependable. I was certain that things would fall apart eventually.

But I was living a richer life than I ever could have dreamed of. It was as if God opened the floodgates and brought me everything all at once. Interestingly enough, I was having a hard time trusting that my happiness would last. I didn't know how to let myself accept all that was coming my way because I was too afraid of losing it.

If I freely accepted the comfortable lifestyle Rick had to offer, I would put myself in yet another place of vulnerability. Loving anyone left my family wide open for disappointment.

I was terrified. Rick was setting the bar awfully high. If he chose to let me go, I would have a long way to fall. Every day I woke up waiting to hear a thud. This fear began to jeopardize my happiness. I almost walked away, thinking that dissolution of the relationship would be the only way to ease my anxiety. It was shocking to discover how difficult it had become for me to find the courage and strength to take a chance on love.

A calm feeling began to develop the instant I was willing to look past my fear. I had been failing to remember the way in which my needs had been met thus far—supernaturally. That my care was now manifesting in a fresh form did not negate the fact that I was still being cared for by the same Trustworthy Hands as before. It might appear that Rick was the one meeting my needs, but there was no escaping the fact that I was now being provided for by the partner God personally handpicked for the task.

I didn't have to fear losing anything. I could rest because God remained in control. If Rick walked away, God would continue to be in control. God was still, and would forever be, my Source. He was simply working through those around me. He was able to bless me because my choices allowed Him to make a way for the right people to enter my life.

Through my relationships with Rick, the Bayles family, Miss Betty, and the Stamford community, I was now witnessing the way connection was meant to work. As I began to let my walls of fear and judgments fall, I began to experience freedom. I found a way to accept love, which brought about a sense of peace and joy. This was the beginning of my living the life God planned for me.

"We can never judge the lives of others, because each person knows only their own pain and renunciation. It's one thing to feel that you are on the right path, but it's another to think that yours is the only path."

Paulo Coelho

Chapter Eight

BLESSINGS

*"What if we truly believed there is a God—
a beneficent order to things, a force that's
holding things together without our conscious
control? What if we could see, in our daily
lives, the working of that force? What if we
believed it loved us somehow, and cared for
us, and protected us? What if we believed we
could afford to relax?"*

Marianne Williamson

Why?

"To feel the Love of God within you is to see the world anew, shining in innocence, alive with hope, and blessed with perfect charity and love."

A Course in Miracles

*A*lmost every person I meet eventually wants to know why I chose to move to Connecticut. I never quite know how to respond. It's not that I don't believe that I made the right choice, but up until now, I simply have had a hard time translating what I've gone through into mere words.

After Tommy's death, I could feel myself being comforted from the inside, something I've found very difficult to describe. During my most desperate moments, I could sense a quiet Supporter encouraging me to hold on. I continually found myself being reassured that all would work out to my benefit.

This is when the shift began to occur in the way I viewed reality. I came to see the spiritual world as being more dependable than the physical one. Instead of wanting all the answers, I began to accept guidance. Instead of understanding God's plan for my life, I began to let Him be in charge of guiding me through it. That's why I chose to take such a risk and move my family to Connecticut. Deep down, I really didn't feel like I was taking a risk at all.

Coincidence?

"Live for today, but hold your hands open to tomorrow. Anticipate the future and its changes with joy. There is a seed of God's love in every event, every unpleasant situation in which you may find yourself."
Barbara Johnson

*E*ven though we had been together only a short time, I felt as if I had known Rick my entire life. It was obvious to more than just me that he and I were destined to be together. In less than three months, Rick's friends wanted to know how long it would be before we said "I do." Some went so far as to wonder what was taking us so long.

This being said, one can only imagine my surprise the day I came to work and overheard customers talking about my new boyfriend.

"I couldn't believe he bought that house in the first place."

"I know. What's he planning to do with all that space?"

"Only Rick would tear down a perfectly good home."

When I inquired about their conversation, I learned that Rick had purchased a fairly large home about two years prior. They all agreed that the house might have needed a little work, but they each viewed Rick's improvements as a bit excessive.

According to the story, Rick tore the entire house apart and uprooted hundreds of rocks and trees outside. It was hard for anyone to understand his reasons for clearing off an entire acre of wooded land.

Rick hadn't made it through the door before I asked him why he never mentioned his home. He looked at me quizzically saying, "I never mentioned it?" After apologizing, he proceeded to explain that his omission was a mere oversight. The remodeling had simply taken a back seat to more important matters. Giving me a sideways glance, Rick pointed out that he'd been a bit preoccupied the past few months with me and the kids.

Rick warned that the house wouldn't be much to look at, but I was welcome to come see for myself. He had a meeting with a contractor later in the day. We could pick up the kids and bring them along for the ride.

When we pulled into the ripped-up driveway, I could see that the entire property had been cleared, leaving only mud and rocks in its wake. I didn't know whether to be shocked or impressed by the recent renovations. Kaden and Anistyn didn't have any reservations. My children had the time of their lives crawling up and over uprooted boulders the size of forts.

Aside from the state of the yard, the outside of the house seemed serene. From the front, it looked like a quaint single-level ranch. From the back, the house was much larger than one could see at first. A good portion of the home was cleverly contained in the lower level only visible from the rear.

The house was located in a beautiful neighborhood and, despite the disruption Rick's jackhammers and large trucks had brought over the past couple of years, his neighbors were very welcoming and seemed anxious to have him move in. I suspect that much of their tolerance was due to the fact Rick had begged forgiveness by personally delivering flowers, wine, and baskets of food to his neighbors.

Rick brought me in through a garage that opened up to a basement. From there I could see that the house had been completely gutted. There were no walls, no insulation, and no sheetrock—just newly framed rooms waiting to be made whole.

We walked into a large open space that would eventually be the second living area. The far wall was lined with windows exposing what I was told would eventually be a stone deck surrounded by rock wall and waterfall.

The far side of the game room would house built-in cabinets designed specifically for a big-screen TV. The woodwork would then continue to wrap around to encompass a bar with an aquarium set behind for the backdrop. A small bedroom, full-size bath, and laundry room left Rick with the future possibility of turning the lower level into a fully functioning apartment if the need ever presented itself.

The main floor was just as bare as the first, though I could see that the entire area was full of potential. Windows had been installed the length of the back of the house, exposing what would eventually be a large deck. The master bedroom had a beautiful walk-in closet as well as a private balcony overlooking a waterfall out back. A spiral staircase to the stone patio below added the perfect finishing touch.

Rick explained that he had not intended to do this much work on the home when he bought it. It just so happened that every repair led to even bigger underlying problems. Thanks to everything falling apart, he was now able to build whatever he wanted.

It all started when Rick discovered water in the basement. He soon realized that the only way to solve the problem permanently would be to waterproof the house from the outside in. So he brought in heavy machines to break through the massive rock and create a four-foot trench around the perimeter of the home.

Once he was able to stop the water from coming in, he was then forced to gut the basement from floor to ceiling to prevent the development of mold. While opening up the basement, he found himself crushing the old copper pipes with his bare hands. That's when he accepted the need for new plumbing.

From there, Rick tried to put the basement fireplace to use to dispose of leftover scrap wood. The moment he lit the fire, smoke began to billow out from the exterior sides of the fireplace walls, covering the floor with yellow-hot embers. Smoke quickly filled the house while Rick frantically put out the flames. In his aggravation, he kicked the fireplace and watched the entire chimney crumble to the ground, leaving a pile of bricks to be carried away by hand.

Everything went downhill from there: old plugs exposed faulty wiring, chipped paint revealed rotting wood, tearing down one wall necessitated tearing down two. Rick realized he would save money by gutting everything and starting from scratch.

Most people would be devastated to discover that they had to tear down a newly purchased home. Not Rick. He simply rolled up his sleeves and found a way to fix the problems. He never once complained about the cost or how much extra work he had to do. He wanted things done right, and he was willing to work tirelessly to make it happen.

As we talked, I could see that the passion this man was pouring into his home mirrored the intensity he showed in every other area of his life. Just being near him left me feeling a sense of relief—not because of what he had been able to accomplish, but because I knew he would never intentionally let me down.

Rick had spent the last twenty years of his life living in a small condo to save money so he could eventually buy a bigger home. He worked hard for what he wanted, and he would never quit, even when everything around him fell apart.

I wondered why on earth Rick would choose to buy a large home that would require so much upkeep and responsibility. Turns out he had been searching the market for years for a multi-family, not a single-family, investment. He had planned to rent out the larger house to a family while he quietly kept to himself—and lived rent-free—in an attached apartment.

He hadn't been interested in this house when the realtor first mentioned it, but, after the initial walk-through, and against his better judgment, Rick felt a strong urge to buy the house. As he went outside to have a moment alone, he began to pray for guidance. He admitted that he didn't need a house this size and had absolutely no good reason for moving ahead. After praying for clarity and peace, he knew without question what to do. For reasons he still doesn't fully understand himself, he immediately walked back inside and purchased the home on the spot.

Inconsequential?

"The reason people find it so hard to be happy is that they always see the past better than it was, the present worse than it is, and the future less resolved than it will be."

Marcel Pagnol

*B*y summer, Rick and I had become inseparable. And, things at work were beginning to look up as well.

I was finally given the green light to move ahead and update the showroom's inventory. Corporate was sending me to the Dallas Market Center for the annual lighting exhibition, with the goal to bring in updated products to help get the showroom up and running effectively.

Since my parents were in the lighting business too, I would be a fool not to pair up with them and take advantage of their expertise.

Because Rick had yet to meet my family, we decided to make a vacation of it. The kids and I flew out first. Friends took care of Kaden and Anistyn so I could focus on business. After the Dallas Market, Rick came out to enjoy the hot Texas sun. I dragged Rick all over the Dallas/Fort Worth area, making sure he received a good dose of Mexican food and margaritas. He met both my family and Tommy's, and was a hit with everyone.

Anistyn had a cold and was very tired at the end of each day. Rick did everything he could think of to keep her happy while we toured the Metroplex. Ice cream, cake, and balloons were on permanent rotation. The kid was a walking sugar bowl. I'll never forget him trying to carry her while suffocating in the hundred degree plus heat.

Our last night in Dallas, Rick was trying to get a very tired family back to the hotel. As he was fighting to change lanes, the kids' balloons in his face, he looked at me and smiled. "What happened to me? Last year at this time, I was driving ninety down the parkway in a Corvette. Now I'm driving a minivan through downtown Dallas with balloons in my face and tissue stuffed in my pockets. I couldn't be happier."

Introducing Rick to people and places in my previous life somehow helped solidify things. It was comforting to have him accepted and to see Tommy's family, as well as my own, happy for me. The only part that felt incomplete was the absence of my old friends.

The companions I had grown up with were a huge part of who I had become. Even our disagreements helped mold me into the woman I am today. We taught each other how to drink, smoke, swear, and drive. We shared the buying of our first homes and the births of our babies. But I'm afraid I took how important they were to me for granted.

My lack of devotion to my Texas friends let something very valuable slip through my fingers. I missed them all more than I had been willing to admit. Our disagreements seemed trivial considering what carrying on without them cost me.

At this point, though, I didn't know how to mend the bridges. I had no idea if my friends would even let me. I also wasn't sure that it would be a good idea to open up old wounds.

I could have called, but I didn't feel right about it. I could have written a letter, but I could never get the right words down on paper. I did nothing because I could never settle on an approach. I finally decided to let go and give my burden over to God.

Weeks later, I received a call from my old friend Teresa saying that she hadn't been able to get me off her mind. Neither of us knew why we allowed things to unfold the way they had, but all she wanted was to lay the past aside so we could once again be involved in each other's lives. The conversation wasn't long, and the relationship didn't instantly go back to the way it had been two years prior, but the door had been pushed open.

Do I believe God instigated this conversation on my behalf? Absolutely. Without fail, my prayers have a way of opening windows and turning my wishes into reality. With God's intervention, one way or another, I always achieve.

Betrayal?

"Such a person has no interest, whatsoever, in what is done or what is not done. A Self-realized person does not depend on any body (except God) for anything."

Bhagavad Gita

*W*e had been back from Dallas for almost two months, and I had yet to receive a single item from my market orders. Numerous calls to corporate headquarters did not yield answers on what had happened to my inventory.

Once I did finally get in touch with someone, I was told to be in Boston the following week and come hungry because lunch would be waiting. We would discuss our next plan of action, and I should be finished up in time to miss the heavy traffic on the drive back to Connecticut.

I showed up hungry to find no food in sight. Instead of discussing improvements, I was informed of the change in direction our company had decided to take. Seems I had been sent to Dallas on a wild-goose chase, and my product orders were never placed. In fact, at no time were they even considered. My boss never intended to invest more money in the showroom. He had made the decision to shut the business down months prior.

I was given three months notice. The only way to receive my severance pay would be to go back and clean things up, get rid of as much inventory as possible, and tactfully fire all my employees in a way that would convince them to stay until we closed the doors for good. I was sent home hungry and expected to go back to do the impossible.

Truthfully, I was taken aback by the news. I was frustrated that I really hadn't been given the tools or the opportunity to do the job I had wanted to do. In spite of all this, I wasn't extremely upset.

I had no idea what direction my life would take, but I wasn't overly stressed about the details. I was actually beginning to worry that there was something wrong with me for not getting worked up over being fired.

I continued to feel a calm reassurance despite the fact that this was not a logical time to feel at peace. My mind kept churning, but my other senses took over to reassure me that I would be fine. Deep down, I felt secure in knowing that everything would work out, one way or another, for my very best interest.

This was when I recognized the most significant change in me. I wasn't at peace simply because things had begun to go my way. I wasn't happy because everything was good in my life. I wasn't secure because I had a good job to turn to. I was at peace because I had undergone a life-altering transformation.

I was no longer the Kerie of old. I had gone beyond being ruled by my circumstances and wasn't overwhelmed by stressful situations anymore. I wouldn't be held captive by the choices other people made. Once and for all, I had been set free.

I had every reason to be upset. I was going to have to walk in and lay off great workers, people who turned down other jobs because I had talked them into working for me. Not one of them deserved this kind of treatment.

This situation wasn't fair, but I was going to have to make the most of circumstances as they arose. I knew that somehow this state of affairs was helping to improve my life.

I felt very sad and a bit lost, but underneath it all was a calm I could not explain. I was certain that my employees and I would end up on our feet and move on to bigger and better things.

Luck?

"Once you become aware that the main business that you are here for is to know God, most of life's problems fall into place of their own accord."

J.I. Packer

*N*ew management took over the supply house while I went about letting everyone in my department go. I did work out a way to keep two employees, which helped ease my guilty conscious.

Instead of being bitter or angry, I began to open myself up to new possibilities. The reality was that my showroom had never been able to offer customers the right kind of merchandise for their homes and budgets. Because of this, ninety percent of all my sales came from catalogue orders—not an ideal situation, but one that had been effective. Most of my customers happily walked away referring me to their neighbors and friends.

It dawned on me that I didn't need a showroom to be successful. I could continue to service the same builders, homeowners, and decorators without having to work for someone else. I knew then that my job had actually been preparing me for my next phase in life—to be a business owner.

From the moment my children were born, I yearned to have the opportunity to spend more time with them. With absolutely no effort on my part, this dream was coming true. God had been well aware of my subconscious fantasies and had been subtly working behind the scenes to bring them to fruition.

My relationship with Rick further helped the situation. Being an electrician made it easier for him to help me find clients. His customers needed lights, and he was able to refer them to a lighting designer.

The last day on the job was not the end of the world, after all. That was the day my schedule opened up, and I was able to start living the life I had been dreaming of. My children were able to come first. I was available for weekend games and after-school activities. I was able to stay home during stormy weather. Losing my job turned out to be one of the best things that ever happened to me.

Fate?

"You know you're in love when you can't fall asleep because reality is finally better than your dreams."

Dr. Seuss

On Labor Day weekend, Rick planned to take me and the kids on a quick trip to Rehoboth Beach. He thought we would enjoy staying by the water where we could enjoy the boardwalk, live music, rides, and plenty of cotton candy and ice cream.

He was right. There was never a shortage of activity, and the weekend was a blast. We didn't stop from the moment we arrived. The kids were trying to make the most of their last day of summer vacation, so we spent the entire day at the beach and most of the night on boardwalk amusement rides. By the time late evening rolled around, I was exhausted and ready to call it a night.

On the walk back to the hotel, Rick decided one last turn down the beach would be fun. I didn't agree. The kids would be covered in sand. I would never have the energy left to get them bathed. The only place I wanted to be was asleep.

Rick's persistence won out, and we veered off toward the water to take a moonlit stroll on the sand. As I suspected, Kaden and Anistyn ran ahead to jump in the water while Rick and I stayed behind.

Needless to say, I was not happy and made it very clear to Rick that he would now be in charge of the children's bath time. He laughed, telling me that he always wanted to be around to help me clean up the messes. At first I was too tired to pay much attention, but he got my interest when he finished by saying, "I would love to be a permanent part of this adventure."

I turned to look at him and noticed he had gotten down on one knee. I was so caught off guard that I couldn't wrap my mind around what he was actually doing. I don't think I heard him ask me to be his wife. My only proof that he did, in fact, pop the question was the ring he pulled out of his pocket.

Rick asked me to marry him on a moonlit beach. I could hear the crashing of the waves and my children laughing in the distance, everything coming together to make this a perfect moment. I can honestly say I was no longer tired. Without hesitating I said "Yes."

Misfortune?

"Anyone can give up, it's the easiest thing in the world to do. But to hold it together when everyone else would understand if you fell apart, that's true strength."

Anonymous

*S*eems the only person surprised by our engagement was me. Most people were more astonished that we waited so long. Funny, nine months didn't seem like such a stretch in my eyes.

From this point on, things started moving very fast. We set a wedding date for October, my lease would be up in December, and Rick was working from morning till night trying to ensure we would have a place to live.

At first we weren't going to have much of a wedding. Both of us are very simple people and we wanted things as easy as possible, but we didn't think that would be fair to the children. We settled on a compromise that would make things fun for them and easy for us—a destination wedding set on a cruise to the Bahamas. The Majesty of the Sea would leave from Miami carrying about sixty of our closest family and friends.

Things didn't exactly turn out as planned. Just before our wedding party was due to fly into southern Florida, hurricane Wilma made her debut. She wasn't gentle either, bringing tornadoes along for the ride. Power was out for two to three weeks, downtown Miami looked like a war zone, and airports were shut down indefinitely. Cruise ships were running, but how would we catch a flight from New York to Miami to board the cruise ship?

Most of the wedding guests' flights were due to land the day before we set sail. I previously arranged for everyone to stay in the same hotel, where we planned to have a large pre-wedding dinner for the entire group.

Unfortunately, there was no power, no flights, and no way to contact the hotel. All our friends were calling Rick to find out what we were going to do.

Our travel agent finally reached the hotel and learned that it would accommodate us if we could get to Miami. On the downside, the hotel had no electricity and no hot water—not an ideal situation for a bride preparing for her big day.

Rick was worried that this setback was going to be too much for his soon-to-be blushing bride. Much to his surprise, he found I was actually enjoying watching the activity. Apparently I was the only one not feeling a sense of panic. I told myself that we could always rent a bus or van and drive everyone to Miami if the airport situation didn't change. In the meantime, our travel agent was able to locate and move all our guests to the one hotel possessing power and running water.

If we had to drive down by ourselves, I was confident that we would make it one way or another. I would be disappointed if our friends were either unable to make a flight or unwilling to drive, but I wasn't going to let it ruin my day.

Most of the panic and worry proved unnecessary. Airline transportation to Miami started back up the day of our flight. Everyone planning to go on the cruise was able to make it down in time. Once we arrived in Miami, we had an entire hotel almost exclusively to ourselves.

A couple of Rick's friends thoughtfully took it upon themselves to find a working restaurant where they booked dinner reservations for our guests. They further surprised us by having a caravan of limousines waiting outside our hotel to take everyone to a lovely dinner.

We reserved a large tour bus to take the wedding guests out to port the following day. Before our departure, I received a message from the wedding planner that the storm damage had closed every florist in town. There was no way to make my bouquet or cake topper.

This seemed like the smallest of our worries. I could get married without a bouquet. All I wanted was to safely get on the ship.

Rick was far less satisfied. As we were leaving the hotel, he went back inside to ask each one of the men to casually swipe a flower from the different arrangements around the hotel. Once they all met on the bus, the guys went about grouping the flowers together, making bouquets for me; my sister, who was my maid of honor; and my daughter, who was my flower girl.

I wasn't presented with the arrangements until just before the wedding. I must say the guys did a fabulous job. Though I later ended up with a yellow stain on my wedding dress from the pollen, I think those bouquets were my favorite part of the entire wedding.

Once we arrived at port, the cruise ship management took over and made Rick's and my life as simple as possible. We had a beautiful suite with a view. We later tied the knot standing in the middle of an Eighties-style disco ballroom, surrounded by the people we love most.

Thanks to Hurricane Wilma, the catering companies were limited on food, but we still were given a feast fit for a king. The wedding cake was supposed to be topped with flowers; due to the shortage, however, the bakery had to improvise. What they came up with was the ugliest contraption known to man—hard spike-shaped icing that looked like the back of a dragon coming up out of the sea. I don't know what they were thinking, but at least it was edible and good for a laugh.

As it turns out, the thing I remember most about my wedding day was the imperfection of it all. It appeared to be chaotic and stressful, but really it was spontaneous and full of lasting memories.

Prearranged?

"Man finds it hard to get what he wants, because he does not want the best. God finds it hard to give, because He would give the best and the man will not take it."

George McDonald

When the cruise was over, my mother took Kaden and Anistyn back to Connecticut so Rick and I could spend the next two weeks island hopping in Hawaii. I found myself sky diving over the north shore of Oahu after a morning of swimming with the sharks. I attended my first luau and zip-lined over the trees in Kauai. We toured Hawaii's live volcanoes by helicopter and swam with the dolphins afterward. In Maui we enjoyed the beautiful view up the Road to Hana, unwound on awe-

inspiring black beaches, and found ourselves scuba diving with nine-hundred-pound sea turtles.

Altogether, the wedding and honeymoon made for a
three-and-a-half week vacation. Once the time came to
come home, we were both ready to get back.

We arrived to happily discover that construction
had been going around the clock while we were away.
The house was just about ready for us to move in. If
things remained on schedule, we would actually be
spending our first Christmas together in our new
home.

As things began to calm down, I was able to sit back
and see everything that God had done for me. My life
was almost unrecognizable. Three years prior to this, I
had been a devastated widow. Now I was not only re-
married, but had started my own business. I was happy,
and my life was full of promise.

During the final walk-through on the house, I was
reminded of the thoughts that were going through my
mind the day I sold the home Tommy and I lived in together. I remember being comforted by that small Voice
inside my head saying that everything I loved would be
given back to me beyond measure if I would only remain faithful to follow God's guidance.

I remembered crying while saying goodbye to Texas, my corner whirlpool tub, my custom cabinets, walk-
in closets, vaulted ceiling, and professionally landscaped
yard. I didn't think it would be possible for me to ever
replace those things again.

Little did I know that, at that very moment, my future
husband was buying a home and preparing it specifically

for the future needs of our family. Everything I lost would come back to me tenfold—my home, my family, my friends, my possessions, and most importantly, my happiness.

With this in mind, I began to look at my finished home in awe. My crown moldings were back and better than before. I not only had one whirlpool tub, now my children had one as well. Now they also had not only a small fenced-in backyard, but a large play area complete with a basketball hoop, trampoline, two story-furnished playhouse, and a rubber-mulched park area. I not only had a better-designed walk-in closet, but one that doubled as a second laundry room for convenience. My children had their own custom-designed bedrooms given for privacy, and my kitchen cabinets boasted top-of-the-line appliances and granite countertops.

My marriage, the house, the traveling, and the material assets that were now a part of my new life were not the reasons for my new-found happiness. My willingness to find happiness without the material gain was what opened the door for everything else to fall into place. I believe that, by trusting God and allowing Him to direct my path, I was led to abundance in every single area of my life. Everything on the outside was a result of what had taken place on the inside.

I did not create any of this on my own. Every blessing in my life was given to me by God. God was not rewarding me; He was simply expressing His love for me.

"God is a good God and He gives good things to his children. No matter who has denigrated you or how much pain you've experienced in life, no matter how many setbacks you have suffered, you cannot allow yourself to accept that as the way life is supposed to be. No, God has better things in store for you. You must reprogram your mind with God's word; change that negative, defeated self-image, and start seeing yourself as winning, coming out on top. Start seeing that marriage as restored. See your business as flourishing. See your children as enjoying the good things of God. You must see it through your eyes of faith, and then it will begin to happen."

Joel Olstean

Chapter Nine

LIVING

"How can we know ourselves? Never by reflection, but only through action. Begin at once to do your duty and immediately you will know what is inside you."

Johann Wolfgang von Goethe

Be Authentic

"We have to keep evolving as people and keep it fresh. Life has its twists and turns, and being comfortable in your skin and loving yourself is the best way to get through life."

Jesse Garza

A life filled with promise is not necessarily void of adversity. That was never more obvious than during the first two years of my marriage. I'll be the first to admit that I married a wonderful man. That being said, the two of us have been known to go a few rounds when it comes to disagreements.

It was the little things that took the most getting used to. We had our hands full trying to settle into our new family role with the children. Both my dog and cat retaliated when Rick refused to let them continue sleeping in my bed. They started peeing all over the new house. I finally had to medicate the poor cat with Prozac, not just to save the carpet, but my marriage as well.

Unlike his previous home, Rick proved to be meticulously clean when it came to this one. He was going nuts trying to keep the house in top form; he was constantly scrubbing the kid's handprints off the walls and trying to keep food off the floor. I can't tell you how many times I heard him mumble that he was the only person in our house who knew how to turn off the lights and television. Rick even debated having the interior walls repainted after the first month.

Our schedules rarely meshed. Rick had been accustomed to living the carefree bachelor life, coming and going as he pleased. He not only continued playing hockey, but he supported two separate baseball teams in his remaining spare time. Needless to say, this didn't go over too well with me. Given the kids, animals, sports, and sleep deprivation, things at our house were quite chaotic.

After a little give and take on both parts, we eventually found a good compromise and began to settle in. However, our biggest challenge came in the form of our third child. If Rick thought he married a difficult woman before we started in vetro fertilization, he hadn't seen anything yet. My past mood swings were child's play compared to what was about to come.

I had no intention of having another child after Anistyn. Tommy and I had two beautiful children and felt our family was complete. I chose to have my tubes tied as a form of birth control. If I had a crystal ball, I might have chosen differently, but who could have guessed I would become a widow seven weeks after the operation?

Rick's one request was that I try to give him another child. For me, a fertility specialist was the only way it would happen. Little did either of us know how dramatically these treatments would affect me. Rick soon found himself injecting me with daily dose of hormones and emotional overload.

My husband didn't understand why I couldn't get it together. I was finding it very difficult trying to cope with an unsympathetic spouse on top of my out-of-control hormones. Nothing and no one were safe from my erratic behavior.

To make things worse, the fertility treatments were not going as planned. Two of my eggs did grow healthy enough for implant, but once it came time for the pregnancy test, my results were inconclusive. Seems my hCG levels were not high enough for me to be considered pregnant. Nor were they low enough for the implantation to have been considered a failure.

Without going into a long fertility discussion, I'll explain that I had to stay on track with daily injections while waiting to see if something positive happened. I was warned that the chances of my pregnancy actually making it were less than ten percent.

Over the next two weeks, my hGC levels continued to elevate, but not enough for me to claim victory. Every other day I walked into the fertility clinic, gave blood, and waited seven to eight hours for the doctor to call back with the same results: pregnant but most likely not with a healthy fetus.

This went on for the first two weeks of my pregnancy, during which time I stayed on the couch, shut the curtains, and cried in the dark. Rick tried a few times to pull me out from under the covers, but it was no use. I preferred to keep hidden while I waited out the day anticipating the doctor's call.

Finally, an ultrasound confirmed that there was a viable fetus. But, my levels were still too low to consider our child out of the woods. I was told to prepare myself for the worst. More than likely, there would be no heartbeat, and the pregnancy would have to be terminated.

I say all this, not to go into a fertility lesson, but to explain why I was a horrible person to be around during this time. I was full of depression, anxiety, rage, and fear. I did believe that God had everything under control, but I did not know if that meant this child was going to survive. I was not ready to come to terms with the idea that my baby might not make it. I didn't try to candy coat my bad attitude, either. It was simply beyond me to change how I felt or reacted. Life was throwing me punches that were too difficult for me to smile and play nice through.

So I nurtured myself by granting myself permission to react honestly. I wasn't planning to stay in this frame of mind indefinitely, but for now, I needed to be patient with my emotions while I found a way to cope with the situation.

My pregnancy did finally end successfully. To make a long story short, at twenty-three weeks, numerous bleeding episodes forced me to remain in the hospital on bed rest. My mom had to come up from Texas to take care of my family while my unborn daughter and I stayed hospitalized for the next three months. Our ordeal came to an end once an emergency C-section brought my daughter Ashtyn into the world five weeks premature.

We were finally able to bring our feisty little girl home two weeks later. She had started off fighting to get into this world, and she has remained strong-willed ever since.

Coming home to three children after months in the hospital was yet another difficult time in my life. I appreciate and love my kids with all of my heart. But sometimes they drive me crazy. I'm human. I cry, I scream, and I throw bigger fits than the kids now and then. Life gets to me, and I'm okay with that. I'm not always happy with my behavior, but I'm doing the best I can, and I love myself for the job I do. I don't have to pretend that things don't go wrong or that every day is a walk in the park. Most days aren't.

Be Carefree

"Don't wish it were easier, wish you were better. Don't wish for fewer problems, wish for more skills. Don't wish for less challenges, wish for more wisdom."

Earl Shoaf

Almost every day, I encounter a situation where stress tries to take control of my life. I immediately remind myself that stress equals unhappiness. When I feel stressed, I know I don't have my head in the right place.

One of the biggest stresses for my family is money. Not only have we undergone extensive costs remodeling our home, but Rick's expenses skyrocketed when we became a family. My poor husband jumped from being a debt-free bachelor to having to support a wife, three children, and a mortgage, literally overnight.

Most of this stress rides on my husband. Ultimately, though, any kind of worry affects the entire family, especially when finances are involved. Because I am no longer working to help offset our expenses, I begin to stress over the fact that I am powerless to make a difference.

As soon as I sit down to pay bills and see things are getting tight, I instantly let myself imagine the worst-case scenario. My credit score will be ruined, we're going to lose the house, my husband is going to come home furious, my marriage is going to crumble, my family will end up on the streets.

Eventually, I start feeling sick and irritable and make everyone around me feel stressed as well. Before I know it, the entire family is on edge. The kids are worried they won't be taken care of. Rick's angry because we spend too much money. I'm angry because I can't control the situation.

This is usually when it's time to remember two very important details. One, all the drama I have created came from an illusion. I jumped to dire conclusions on the basis of a single bill going unpaid.

I turn this around by simply taking a better look at my true circumstances. Nine times out of ten, I'm sitting in a beautiful office, wearing warm clothes, sipping a cup of my favorite green tea, and enjoying a nice snack. My needs for the moment are definitely met. I have no one to blame but myself if I make myself miserable imagining a destitute future.

Second, I remind myself that I am not powerless at all. No, I can't bring home money at this time, but I can help lower the amount of stress my family feels. The way I choose to look at our circumstances determines how those around me will see them. I have much power because it is my faith and courage that keeps everyone calm during difficult times. If I remain steady, I can help my family keep the right perspective, too. So I take whatever action I can: tighten the budget, turn down the heat, find ways to stay home and have fun for free. I may have to pay a late fee now and then, but, without fail, my bills are covered each month.

I have stated many times that I don't consider money to be my provider, that my Provider is the One who is able to move money around. Yes, I do have to be responsible and diligent, but as I am being diligent, so is God. I stay focused on my blessings and wait in expectation to see how tomorrow is going to unfold.

Be Generous

"Let no one ever come to you without leaving better and happier. Be the living expression of God's kindness: kindness in your face, kindness in your eyes, kindness in your smile."

Mother Teresa

The more generous I am with my time and money, regardless of how little I may have, the happier I am. My fulfillment is fueled by my willingness to give.

I thought raising a family and nurturing a healthy marriage were what I was meant to do in life. Something inside of me kept calling for more, however. I knew God was stirring me up for a reason. I had a strong desire to want to help not only my family but all those around me. I knew without a doubt that changes were inevitable.

What would my new challenge be? I felt extremely uneasy talking to people about God. I wasn't involved enough at church to feel comfortable teaching Sunday school or talking in front of groups. I had no background that would lead me toward a therapeutic career. I had no skill that would help me do much of anything other than sell lights.

That's when I began to focus on what brought me the most gratification for the moment—giving. The more I gave of myself, the more clearly I could see how gratifying it was to reach out and offer a helping hand.

I began to fulfill my desire by opening up my home to those around me. My environment was a blessing and I found ways to share that blessing with my family and friends.

From that moment on, there was never a stranger to walk through my front door. We welcomed our neighbors at any time. I learned to make dinners that would feed large groups of people in case I had last-minute guests, and I happily saved any leftovers for another night. Sometimes I would even come home to find neighbors in the backyard throwing balls to my dog while their kids played in my children's playhouse.

It was fairly typical for me to have twelve boys in the basement and four little girls upstairs trying to get to sleep. My children have been taught not to leave others out, and following through with this lesson challenged my husband and me to come up with ways to creatively entertain large groups of kids. Rick has gone so far as to bring home buckets of ice cream and toppings, cover the dining room floor with tarps, and surprise the kids with banana split nights.

Yes, we get tired and want space to ourselves. When our batteries run low, we take time to be alone. But when we do have a house full of children, we find that they are respectful, do as we ask, and help us clean up afterward.

Opening our home like this is a calling of mine, and my family is very supportive and comfortable with it. That's the reason it works for us. I believe that, when we answer to a Higher Call, even when we aren't fully able to understand the reasoning behind our actions, we can rest assured that the details will fall into place.

This is my way of answering what I feel is God's calling for me to reach out to people. Because I pay attention to God, my home is filled with happiness and laughter. Being helpful doesn't require that I try and help people solve their problems. I'm most effective when I simply reach out and offer unconditional love to everyone around me.

Be Influential

"It is finally when you let go of what people expect you to be and people's perceptions of you that you're able to be the version of yourself that you're supposed

to be—like in God's eyes. It doesn't matter if you're half crazy, or eccentric, or whatever it is - you have to be true to who you were born to be."

Gwyneth Paltrow

The more I experimented with the idea that helping others did not require words but positive actions, the more I could see how many opportunities there were for me to be inspiring.

For me, the only way to help uplift others was to focus mainly on myself. I could change the world by making my life a light of love that held the power to offer my neighbors hope. I no longer wanted to wait to see miracles take place. I wanted to be the miracle myself.

I witnessed change in people of all ages once I accepted and loved them unconditionally. Lives transformed when I led by example and let those around me see actions that proved a better way. I let my fulfillment be a light guiding people to find the truth for themselves. I became convinced that my love could and would be transformational.

My desire has never been to convert those around me to my way of thinking or to change people's minds about their beliefs. I believe wholeheartedly that the way to know the truth about God and our salvation is by first trusting in something greater than oneself. We can then follow our own hearts to find Truth individually.

With this in mind, the best way for me to become a positive influence was to first create an environment where any issue could be discussed. The first step was to relinquish fear and shame and bring my own pain out in the open. If I was going to create a safe environment for others, I had to be willing to listen while withholding judgment.

My home has become a place of healing and peace. Friends feel loved within our walls and walk away refreshed and uplifted. People drop by to simply sit on the balcony, have a glass of wine, and relax. There is much to be said about creating a healing environment.

To help others find happiness, I see my job as simply to be an example to follow. By doing this, I have been able to witness God's love reach out to help people even when they are completely unaware of His presence. Many times I've watched suffering slowly ease while the recipient sits quietly taking no action whatsoever.

The only part I have in the healing process is to love; God does the rest. My faith and compassion simply open a door so that people can find healing on their own.

Be Open

"Around here, however, we don't look backwards for very long. We keep moving forward, opening up new doors and doing new things, because we're curious… and curiosity keeps leading us down new paths."

Walt Disney

*W*ith all my heart, I wanted the purpose of my life to be helping people by somehow lifting them to a place of hope. This longing was actually a sign telling me that my soul had a job it was ready to get to work accomplishing.

While growing up, I remember language being my worst subject. I couldn't write a creative paper to save my life, and it took parental nagging to get me to read a book. I had no patience for sitting still and couldn't imagine being pressured to read or write all day.

It's funny now to think how I could never understand the desire to pursue a writing career—the isolation, monotony, low pay, and the unpredictably of it all never called to me. I found the entire process dull, boring, and of no interest whatsoever.

I can't tell you how caught off guard I was when I began to feel led to write this book. In fact, I rejected the notion for more than a year. I laughed at the silliness of the idea and thought of the reasons why such a project would be a waste of time: I had no training, I didn't have the time, I wasn't being practical, and I would be way out of my league.

The more I denied it, the more aware I became of the inevitable. I could do nothing to stop the flow of continual ideas rushing through my head. The only way to slow them down and make sense of my thoughts was to put pen to paper and allow the ideas to flow freely. I even went so far as to buy a voice recorder so I could tape my thoughts while I was driving the car.

In spite of taking these steps, I was still having a difficult time accepting the fact that there was a writer inside of me waiting to be released. The main problem was my fear. I had no one to turn to for help. I didn't know how to get started. Most of all, I feared what others would think of me once they found out that I was crazy enough to try to write a book.

I went through a period when I was extremely frustrated. I was feeling pushed to do something that I didn't know how to accomplish. On top of it all, I had a constant flow of thoughts filtering through my head that I didn't know what to do with.

I would go to church and wish the pastor would approach certain subjects with more depth and clarity. I would then go home and give my husband, or whoever would listen, a rundown of how I didn't understand why people weren't being given some very basic concepts that would help them improve their lives.

That's when I was hit hard with a very enlightening thought: **They weren't saying it because the ideas were not given to them.** These ideas had been given to me, and I was doing nothing productive with the information I had been blessed with. In other words, this was my message, and I needed to quit procrastinating and start sharing it with others.

I knew then that I would eventually write a book. I kept it a complete secret. Not even my husband was aware of my newly budding career. All that I was sure of was that I could no longer deny my calling. My passion had become too strong for me to ignore.

Though I had no idea how to get started, a single passage in a book I was reading, *Think and Grow Rich* by Napoleon Hill, gave me the push I needed to move forward: "No individual has sufficient experience, education, native ability, and knowledge to insure the accumulation of a great fortune without the cooperation of other people."

The author then went on to tell how important it was to stop procrastinating and just get started. I didn't have to have the entire plan mapped out from day one; once I began, the details would unfold. If I was willing to take advantage of the experience, education, native ability, and imagination of other minds, I would start to see things come together.

After reading this, my heart began racing, my palms began to sweat, and I began to cry. I was out of excuses. My Spirit had been trying to get my attention long enough. I didn't know how to fulfill my destiny, but I did know that it was time to get to it. Somewhere out there was a team of people who would be around to help. I had no idea who they were or how I would find them, but deep down I knew that the details would unfold in due time.

Sometimes significant changes can take us by surprise. That's why I've learned that it is so important to watch for signs. My Spirit was communicating to me that it was time to move forward. It can be very difficult to be open to new ideas, especially when they don't seem to fit the mold we have created, but if we are not open, we can never grow.

I've finally figured out that failure is nothing to fear; it is simply an opportunity to try another approach.

Never stop believing in yourself. If you feel something telling you to do more, go for it. You may be surprised to discover that you are capable of accomplishing so much more than you ever dreamed possible.

Be Passionate

"Most people can do extraordinary things if they have the confidence or take the risks. Yet most people don't. They sit in front of the telly and treat life as if it goes on forever."

Philip Andrew Adams

I could feel the resolve the instant I made up my mind to move forward. I soon found out that being a writer and writing were two different things, however. Putting my ideas into a readable format proved to be much more difficult than I ever imagined.

It didn't take long for me to realize that it was time for me to take Napoleon Hill's advice to heart. I had to find a way to surround myself with people who could encourage and help me through this process or I would fail. I had no problem asking for help; the trouble was that I had no idea where to find it.

The only thing I knew for sure was that I wanted to work independently in a private setting. I went to the most logical source, Google, looking for ideas. I was soon sorting through countless names of editors and writing coaches working in my area.

I had no idea what qualities to look for in narrowing down the list. That's when I decided to do what had become very natural for me: I let my Intuition decide. Among the many names, one in particular kept coming to my attention—Gay Walley. She was a published author who lived in Manhattan and worked as an editor and a writing coach on the side. I instinctively knew that she was the one.

It was time now to see if I truly had the passion to move ahead and the will to make the necessary sacrifices to be a success. Would I be willing to dedicate myself one hundred percent to this project?

I would have to be accountable to someone other than myself. This meant sticking to a schedule and writing every day. My home, three kids, self-employed husband, and very busy schedule already demanded my full-time attention. The only way I could do everything successfully would be to get an early start to each day before the rest of my family needed me. Coaching and editing would not be free either. Considering money was tight, it was a big decision to commit a substantial amount of it to my work.

To tell the truth, I didn't analyze the sacrifices too extensively because I didn't want to talk myself out of doing whatever needed to be done. I sent Gay an email stating that though I had no experience with writing, I had a book that needed to be written and was willing to commit myself to working with her right away.

She responded very graciously and suggested that I send some of my work over for review. After reading a few pages of raw notes, she asked if I could have my first chapter ready by the end of the week. We could review and get started from there. Before I had time to talk myself out of it, my first meeting was already set.

The scary part now was revealing my new plans to my husband, who would probably think I had lost my mind.

Thankfully, Rick was supportive from the start. When I told him I wanted to write a book, he told me I'd better get started. I added that I would have to pay an editor and commute to Manhattan weekly to get help with my work. He said that nothing worth doing or having ever came without paying a price. I then broke the news that I was planning to wake up at 4:00 a.m. every day to have quiet time to work in private. That's when he walked out of the room pretending not to hear me.

I protected myself and my work by writing in secret for over a year. I didn't tell anyone other than my husband and children what I was doing because I knew it would be difficult for people to understand and be supportive. This was my way of ensuring that negativity couldn't creep in and discourage me.

I had no idea that choosing to write a book would be such a difficult task! Words never seemed to go on paper the way they appeared in my head. And they didn't seem to make sense to anyone other than me. Nonetheless, I had to see this project through—I had set my mind to it.

I refused to allow myself to become overwhelmed by the amount of work that was ahead of me. I was made well aware of countless horror stories. I knew that most writers fail to ever land an agent or make it to publishing. The ones that do make it can just as easily sit on the shelf and fade away.

Nevertheless, I could not let fear of failure stop me from moving forward. God was willing to invest Himself in me and my work. He could easily align the pieces to ensure my success. But, first, I had to be willing to make the investment of myself. I got out of bed every day reminding myself of where I wanted to go, and I stayed determined to get there.

I was fortunate to have the right kind of support. My connection with Gay proved to be yet one more instance in which my most significant relationships were divinely orchestrated. For reasons I will never understand, from the start Gay could see potential in me and promise in a very juvenile piece of work. She never tried to mold me into something I was not, but allowed my individuality to come forth and to be expressed on the pages.

This is how it went for the next two years of my life. Between caring for three children, following my busy schedule, and waking early to write, I found it very difficult to fit in much time for myself. I was exhausted by 7:30 every night and was in bed by 8:00. My weekends were devoted to meeting with Gay and trying to perfect my work. Writing my book would alter my entire way of life.

During this project, I don't remember a day that I wasn't given the opportunity to reach out and grab hold of my lifeline from God. The more frustrated I became, the more I tried to remember that being faithful did not always ensure instant gratification. I can honestly say that nothing has brought more fulfillment into my life than following my dreams and submitting to the call of my Spirit. It took action and dedication on my part, but the joy and freedom I have experienced have been priceless. I may not have an audience and I may be working for free, but I am being faithful in following my heart.

My passion for life leads me to continue to grow stronger every day. I know what is right, and I know where my heart is guiding me. I am constantly reminded that failure is not an option, that steady progress will lead me to the end of the line.

Spirit communicates Itself in different ways in each of us. My form of expression happens to be writing. It's not important what our chosen path may be. What is important is that we take the time to pursue our destiny with zeal and determination.

Be Supportive

"The unique personality which is the real life in me, I cannot gain unless I search for the real life, the spiritual quality, in others. I am myself spiritually dead unless I reach out to the fine quality dormant in others. For it is only with the god enthroned in the innermost shrine of the other, that the God hidden in me, will consent to appear."

Felix Adler

Too many people believe their life is of little value, as I once did. To those who feel this way, let me say that every person has something to give. Life is meaningful, and there is purpose to be found within us all. Nothing can be done about yesterday. Accepting that makes it easier to focus on today. As we focus on today, we can begin to make the choices that will lead to a better tomorrow.

Everyone in the world makes a difference in one way one or another. It's of no benefit to make harsh judgments that you aren't good enough. Never believe that your life has no purpose. You have meaning. You have a destiny.

Focus on living a life from the heart from here on out. I promise that you will discover your value and purpose. Our Spirit knows the grand scheme of things. Trust that It knows what It is doing and begin to follow.

Any time you look at your life as meaningless, take a moment to consider Tommy. If this book has reached you or made any kind of difference in your life, then his short existence meant a great deal. Tommy thought he was worth so little. He believed he wasn't good enough for me and his children. He was unhappy with himself and chose to rid the world of the burden he believed himself to be.

I know differently. His life, as well as his death, changed me dramatically. I hope he can see the truth now. He did make a difference. His life was worth something.

Keep in mind that you may never know just how your life is influencing others, but trust me when I say that it is. We are all swimming together in the great sea of life. When one is treading poorly, we all suffer.

It's time that we choose to live outside of our own needs. The more we give, the more comes back in return. We are in this not just for ourselves but for each other. Our main goal should be to support one another.

People need to feel protected. They need to feel safe. And they will if we choose to see the best as opposed to the worst, if we don't try and fix them, if we show them understanding and compassion.

I challenge you today to go out and live your life in a way that will make you genuinely happy. Take everything that's inside of you and give it away. Try to uplift someone. Be accepting, and try to see the good in those around you. Keep in mind how you felt at your lowest points and consider how you would have wanted to be treated.

So here it seems I begin again. I give you my mistakes, my trials, my victories, and my blessings. I gladly share all that I've learned in hopes of encouraging you to do the same.

With this book, I once again take a step into the unknown without any guarantee of success. I have no idea where this road will lead. It will require work. It will require patience. It will require faith.

Then why go forward you may ask. The answer, my friend, has already been given. Dr. Wayne D. Dyer says it perfectly, "God speaks to all of us with the same intensity; it's the warriors who hear it." That's what I consider myself, a warrior—and so are you. Listen, and move in peace to your destiny.

God bless.

"I asked God for strength that I might achieve. I was made weak that I might learn humbly to obey. I asked for health that I might do greater things. I was given infirmity that I might do better things. I asked for riches that I might be happy. I was given poverty that I might be wise. I asked for power that I might have the praise of men. I was given weakness that I might feel the need of God. I asked for all things that I might enjoy life. I was given life that I might enjoy all things. I got nothing that I asked for, but everything I hoped for. Almost despite myself, my unspoken prayers were answered. I am, among all men, most richly blessed."

Anonymous